Duck

Duck

Victoria de Rijke

REAKTION BOOKS

Published by
REAKTION BOOKS LTD
33 Great Sutton Street
London EC1V 0DX, UK
www.reaktionbooks.co.uk

First published 2008
Copyright © Victoria de Rijke 2008

Printed and bound in China

British Library Cataloguing in Publication Data
de Rijke, Victoria
    Duck. – (Animal)
    1. Ducks 2. Animals and civilization
    I. Title
    598.4'1

ISBN-13: 978 1 86189 350 5

Contents

Preface

> Nature produces them, contrary to her own laws, in a most extraordinary manner. They are like marsh ducks but smaller. They grow in the guise of growths in the trunks of trees that have been washed up on the beach by the sea. As they grow, they hold onto the trunk with their beaks like seaweed adheres to the wood on the beach. Shells protect them so they can grow freely underneath.[1]

What were these marvels? Ducks in a larval stage? Travelling through Ireland in the twelfth century, Gerald of Wales goes on to explain how over time the ducks become covered by a layer of feathers and drop off into the water or fly into the air. He insists that they feed on the sap from the sea itself, allegedly having seen more than one thousand of these little birds hanging from a tree trunk on the beach, lying under their shells and already formed. Gerald observes that certain bishops and prelates in Ireland eat these creatures during Lent because they are not made of meat.[2]

Did Catholic priests, who had no intention of giving up their meat diets for Lent, invent vegetable ducks? A cunning excuse: birds called 'bernacae' found in large quantities all over Ireland, justifying roast duck dinners all through Lent. In 1597 Gerard's *Herbal* referred to the phenomenon again: the duck's special familiarity and ease on land, air or water offers richly confused interpretation:

> This fowle vnknowen to the Auncients hath no certeine name amongst the Greekes . . . Amonge the Latynes . . . from the branded colour thereof callinge it Branta or Bernicula . . . In France they call it Crabans or Crauant or Oye Nonnette, the Germanes Baumganss, Wiewolanch,

Claude Duret's 'Portrait of tree with rotting branch which produces mould, then living, flying duck', from his *Histoire admirable des plantes et herbes esmervill- ables & miraculeuse en nature* (1605).

and the Scots Clakis. [It] liveth in fresh waters: sometimes aboue and sometimes vnder.

'Sometimes above and sometimes under': that is the prevailing
mystery of duck – existing in between the elements, in between
reality and imagination, unstable creature that it is.

This book begins with a natural history. The term used to
categorize duck – *tribe* – is not used with any other avian family
but is instead found in plant taxonomy, referring us back to the
medieval confusion cited above. We move from what science has

Duret's depiction of a tree from which fish or fowl are made, depending on where they fall.

classified to matters of more slippery duck and human interest, and tell a story which moves from facts on the duck fossil record, problems of taxonomy, habitat, feeding and migration, to the border territories of navigation, sociability, display and sexual behaviours.

Chapter Two examines wild duck hunting, domestication, and how ducks continue to be 'pressed' into social organization. Chapter Three analyses associative human and duck sound and resulting metaphor and music. The discussion of a politicized relationship between ducks and humans is animated by

Disney's Donald in chapter Four, while chapter Five explores duck shapes and entertainment. Chapter Six brings the book to a close with a review of ducks and doctors, ducks and disease, and ducks and meaning.

In a Mexican creation myth a great bird came whirling, and its feathers fell into the water, turning into all the waterbirds of the world. Duck came from one of those feathers. Another tale relates how the Iroquois hero Hiawatha, travelling through Mohawk territory, came to the edge of a great lake. As he was wondering how to cross it, a huge flock of ducks descended on the lake and began to drink the water. When the ducks rose up again, the lake was dry, its bed covered in shells. From these shells Hiawatha made the first wampum beads and used them to unite the tribes in peace.

Waterfowl are part of the sacred story of life, and in Egypt were associated with Isis in bringing forth the sun. In Yoruba creation myth the world began as marsh full of waterfowl, and for the Magyars (the inhabitants of present-day Hungary) the sun god Magyar turned himself into a diving duck and made humans out of sand and seedy muck from the ocean floor. For the Hebrews and many other cultures, duck is associated with immortality. According to Indian legend and the sacred texts of the Brahmins, the world was born out of a cosmic egg, the *Brahmanda*. In the Rig-Veda, the most ancient of Indian religious texts, a duck lays golden eggs on a nest built on the head of a thief, and the Finnish epic Kalevala describes a duck building a nest on the body of Ilmator (daughter of Air) as she lies in the sea. The duck lays eggs that fall and crack open, the yolk forming earth and the rest the heavens, sun, moon, stars and clouds. In ancient thinking, the Celts, Greeks, Egyptians, Hindus and Chinese all believed that the sky was the upper half

The best good-turnes that Fooles can doe us,
'Proove difadvantages unto us.

67

Claus Narr

A. STULTORUM ADIUMENTA NOCUMENTA

NE MERGANTUR

ILLVSTR, XVII.

Book. 4.

In George Wither's *Collection of Emblemes, Ancient & Modern* (1635), an interfering fool inadvertently kills the waterfowl he carries over the river in case they should drown themselves paddling across! The surrounding Latin motto translates as 'The assistance of fools only brings trouble'.

of a cosmic egg. And since ducks live both in the sky and the water and lay eggs, they naturally lend themselves to cosmic interpretation and explanation.

> '*Omnis mundi creatura*
> *Quasi liber et pictura*'
> – *Et hic erit Anas.*[3]

> 'Every creature of this world
> is like a book, a portrait'
> – and this will be Duck.

1 Natural History

If it looks like a duck, and quacks like a duck, we have at
least to consider the possibility that we have a small aquatic
bird of the family Anatidae on our hands.
Douglas Adams, *Dirk Gently's Holistic Detective Agency*

The 151 species collectively known as waterfowl or wildfowl
belong to the class of Aves (birds): order Anseriformes, family
Anatidae and sub-family Anserinae. Anseriformes – the term is
derived from the Latin verb *anas*, to swim – include ducks, geese
and swans and their relatives. Ducks, geese and swans make
up the family Anatidae. Most ducks belong to the sub-family
Anserinae. With a hundred additional sub-species in tribes,
there are probably a total of 250 different forms of ducks. The
species has beaks or bills covered with soft skin, some with a
horny plate or 'nail' on the front, which can curve over the end
like a hook or be shaped like a spatula. The bill is flattened and
has horny teeth, or blade-like lamellae. The front toes are
webbed. Size, plumage and wings vary, from the tiny russet torrent duck *Merganetta armata* to the spectacularly colourful and
large mandarin duck *Aix galericulata*. Consistent duck characteristics are: a broad body, a short tarsis or lower leg set well back,
plumage waterproofed with oil from a gland near the tail, a
'speculum' or area of metallic colouring on the trailing edge of
the wing, a flexible neck with a large preen gland crowned by a
tuft of feathers, and a large external penis in males. Ducks have
worldwide distribution, great diversity of habitat, food sources
and feeding habits, lessening the usual competition between the
species. Though the mallard's (*Anas platyrhynchos*) 'quack' is best

Waterfowl, *Aves aquatica*, or *anseriformes*, includes ducks, geese and swans and other swimming birds, as in this schematic illustration from Jan Comenius's encyclopaedia for children, *Orbis sensualium pictus* (1657).

known, ducks have a huge sound repertoire. They are gregarious, good flyers, swimmers and divers. Their main predator is man.

Although avian taxonomists disagree on the classification of the family Anatidae, most ornithologists place related water-fowl groups into units called *tribes*: *Tadornini* (shelducks), *Tachyerini* (steamer ducks), *Mergini* (scoters, etc.), *Aythyini* (pochards and scaups), *Somateriini* (eiders), *Cairinini* (perching ducks), *Dendrocygnini* (whistling ducks), *Oxyurini* (stiff-tails) and *Anatini* (dabbling ducks).[1] In *Duck* different features of the tribes have been selected to dramatize the remarkable aspects of duck natural history.

THE FOSSIL RECORD: A TRIBE OF ONE

In 1891 *The Catalogue of Fossil Birds in the British Museum* listed a number of duck fossil findings from Essex and the Norfolk Fens in England, and Puy-de-Dôme and elsewhere in France, as well as Switzerland, Germany and New Zealand: tiny pieces of bone

The tribal arrangement for ducks was first proposed by Jean Delacour and Ernst Mayr in 1945, and developed by Paul Johnsgard in 1961.

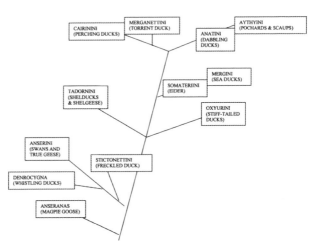

found in cave deposits or rock, with further fragments discovered in North America, China and Europe. The *Animal Life Encyclopedia* identifies the earliest anseriform fossils as *Anatalavis rex* (duck-winged bird king): 'Two bones recovered in New Jersey may date back to the late Cretaceous period (80–50 million years ago), and similar bones found in England helped identify those fossils as possibly duck. The most common anseriform in the fossil record is Presbyornis from the Paleocene and early Eocene' (65–50 million years ago).[2] In January 2005 a partial skeleton of a dinosaur duck, *Vegavis iaai*, was discovered on Vega Island, western Antarctica – though it may be (as a sceptical Professor Alan Feduccia argued) 'an unidentifiable bundle of bones'.[3]

Which begs the question: what is a duck? The pygmy goose is smaller than a duck; the Egyptian goose looks like a duck; and a duck's skeletal character cannot – it is said – be distinguished from that of a goose. In the skull form, a goose is so much like a mallard that no osteological line can be drawn.

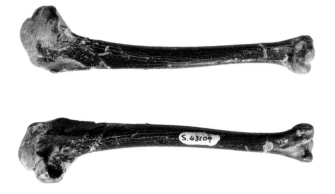

New analysis of duck fossils such as these discovered in New Zealand suggest that *Dendrocheninae* is not real and that its members form part of an expanded *oxyurine* (stiff-tailed) duck tribe.

A tribe of just one species, *Stictonetta naevosa* (freckled duck, gadwall or guall-guall to Australian Aborigines) has affinities with geese and swans but has no near living relatives. Its unpatterned downy young, remarkably primitive syringeal structure and reticulated tarsus all argue strongly for the position that this duck is the sole survivor of a very ancient waterfowl lineage, evolved some 20 million years ago. Covered with mottled dark brown and cream flecked, speckled or 'freckled' feathers, the

Freckled duck (*Stictonetta naevosa*).

drake's bill turns red in the breeding season. It has been described as 'quiet, tame and sleepy, with a voice like the grunt of a Berkshire pig'.[4] It is currently endangered, among the ten rarest birds in the world, and is part of captive breeding programmes between Australia, the US and UK.

Victoria caves in Naracoorte (an Aboriginal word for 'large waterhole') have provided possible duck fossil remains. The latest idea, based on details of the skull, is that they evolved early in the lineage that includes waterfowl. Because of its large skull, some possible carnivorous habits and its probable waterfowl relationships, *Bullockornis* and/or *Dromornis stirtoni* has been nicknamed 'the demon duck of doom'.[5] Yet, of some 15,000 mammals and 6,000 reptiles from Tertiary deposits, palaeontologists say we have fully described only fifteen birds. Where *are* the fossil ducks? Why has a creature common to all continents left so little record?

The simple fact is that fragile bird bones are more easily destroyed by time than those of most animals. There are a few fossil remains of huge extinct geese and swans, and fossil duck fragments from the Miocene (13–11 million years ago) and Pleistocene (11–1.8 million years ago) eras. *Chenornis*, from the mid-Miocene, is a fossil duck said to have affinities with the petrel and pelican, but the *Guide des Fossiles de France* points out the uncertainties:

> Because there is no complete series of duck skeletons, duck taxonomy is subject to guesswork. The oldest certain anatids are the genera Romainvillia Lebedinsky and Cygnopterus Lambrecht from the early Oligocene (34–23 million years BP) of France and Belgium, respectively. These were rather large forms, the size of geese, but of uncertain affinity. Anatids are not common as fossils

until the Neogene (23 million years BP). In many Pliocene (5.5–1.8 million years BP) and Pleistocene freshwater deposits, ducks and geese are the dominant group of birds. If it arose as early as the Cretaceous, the lack of fossils is difficult to understand.[6]

PROBLEMS OF TAXONOMY

The tribe *Tadornini* (shelducks) with its fourteen species is a good example of the categorical confusion around ducks as it either exists alone or includes the *Tachyerini* (steamer ducks). According to Phillips, the duck family Anatidae 'are headed by the Sheldrakes of the Old World',[7] which, depending on your perspective, are either large ducks or small geese. English vernacular names for *Tadorna tadorna* (common shelduck) are St George's duck or sly goose. German and many Scandinavian languages use *brand Ente* or *Gans* (fire-duck or goose), and *Tachyerus pteneres* (flightless steamer duck) is *canard à vapeur* or *oie de plein* (full goose) in French. The Spanish call the species *paro-tarro* (duck jar) and their portraits do in fact feature on many jars from antiquity. There is a fine mosaic of the species in Pompeii and Pliny mentions them breeding in holes on an island off the coast of Apulia. A method of identifying and distinguishing between ducks, swans and geese is argued for in Eykman's *European Anatidae* by size, form or colour of bill and feathering near the tail.[8] The sexes differ little in swans and geese but widely in ducks: in particular, males have more conspicuous plumage.

The taxonomic history of Anatidae began early in English when the naturalist John Ray edited *Ornithologia libri tres* (1676) for Francis Willughby. Considered the beginning of scientific ornithology in Europe, the work included a comprehensive classi-

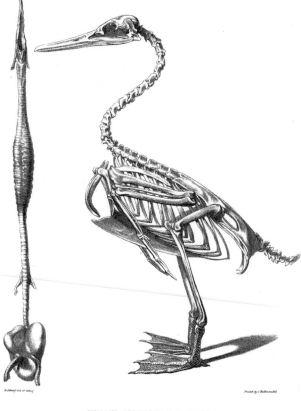

'Mergus Serrator & Trachea' as drawn by the naturalist Thomas Eyton, for *A Monograph on the Anatidæ, or Duck Tribe* (1838).

MERGUS SERRATOR & TRACHEA.
Two thirds the Nat. Size

fication of aquatic birds. Much has been clarified since then, but controversy remains. A rough agreement is that Anatidae comprises 41 genera and 147 species. Most attempts to provide a 'natural' classification – one that best reflects actual evolutionary relationships – are variations on a scheme first proposed by

Delacour and Mayr in 1945. Where earlier classifications had emphasized the association of species at the sub-familial level, this landmark work instead emphasized association at the tribal level. Johnsgard's behavioural studies of the family from 1961 simplified things further into seven sub-families or tribes. Simple species definitions and unequivocal numbers are inadvisable in a highly variable species like duck.

HABITAT

In terms of habitat, ducks can be found anywhere that is wet. Ducks need some sort of wetlands or body of water; the white-headed stiff-tail (*Oxyura leucocephala*) is found on the steppe lakes, Brazilian teal (*Amazonetta brasiliensis*) in the rainforests, African black duck (*Anas sparsa*) in tidal estuaries and mallards (*Anas platyryhnchos*) on your local pond. Ducks are fantastically adaptable, hence their success in numbers. They can live in almost any part of the world in any temperature as long as they have access to water. Constant bathing in good water keeps ducks cool, clean and free of pests; preening also waterproofs and oils soft parts such as feet and bills.

The range of habitat diversity spans the tribe *Mergini*, including true sea ducks like the scoter (*Melanitta*), the torrent duck (*Merganetta armata*), which swims with and against quick-running torrents in rivers and mountain streams, and smews (*Mergus albellus*), introduced to the parks of European cities since 1840. The torrent duck has one species: a fairly rare duck of the Andean mountains, with a torpedo-shaped, streamlined body and spikes on the wings assisting rapidity, and relatively isolated populations between Venezuela and Tierra del Fuego. As Stolzmann observed in 1886, the torrent duck 'dives and swims with incomparable celerity' in its special habitat.[9]

Surf scoter showing their characteristic red beaks and various formations in the skies.

In contrast, the tribe *Mergini* (sea duck) has twenty species, including harlequin (*Histrionicus histrionicus*), also called 'circus duck', because of its colourful harlequin-clown plumage, and 'squealer' or 'sea-mouse', because of its squeaky voice. *Mergini* resemble diving ducks with their large flap-like lobes to the hind toe, long necks and narrow bills, well adapted for agility underwater, diving for (and living off) fish, including catching them under ice. *Bucephala clangula* (called goldeneye because of its markedly bright yellow eyes) is a restless individualist of the *Mergini* tribe with acute sight and hearing, swimming with its head forward as if looking down into the water.

Scoter roam the seas – in fact, the Common or Black Scoter (*Melanitta negrita*, or little black diver) is thought to be the subject of the pre-seventeenth-century belief that *marcreuse* (derived from the French *maigre*, to fast) had their origins in sea-shells or in worms on the rotten wood of shipwrecked ships.

This made them both fish and fowl and therefore suitable eating for fasting periods, as mentioned in the Preface.

Duck habitat is constantly at risk from competitive human interest, and recent research trying to keep the North American and Pacific seas a sustainable habitat and feeding ground for the scoter in the face of the human shellfish farming industry is one example. Scoter are also at risk from the dangers of oil pollution, for great numbers feed in the entrances of crowded harbours where conditions are far from ideal.

Scoters gather in their thousands to feed off the annual herring run off Vancouver Island, British Columbia.

FEEDING AND DIET

In 1838 the ornithologist Thomas Eyron produced his *Monograph of the Anatidae or Duck Tribe.* Species whose names have since disappeared are confidently drawn and described: 'Summer Duck'; 'Spirit Duck', even 'Supercilious Duck'. But like

Vaucanson the automatist, whom I discuss in chapter Four, Eyron was most interested in the workings of the bird: 'The intestinal anatomy of the family Anatidae is characterised by the very great length of the alimentary canal compared to that of the bird: in some instances it is as many as five times its length, even more.'[10] Ducks are eating machines.

In terms of their feeding ecology and diet, surface-feeding ducks either dabble at the surface of the water or mud, swinging their bills, sifting for small invertebrates and plant materials, or 'ending-up' by sticking their heads underwater so far that their tail is the only thing left showing. In this way they can reach the bottom of shallow waters with their bills. Diving ducks can reach greater depths by diving deep below the surface, using their wings to help them swim underwater, though mergansers use only their webbed feet for remarkably quick twists and turns chasing fish. Diving ducks have been caught 40 metres (100 ft) down in the sea in trawl nets.

Ducks eat by using highly specialized (sometimes elongated and spatulate) bills dipped in the water, filtering it and food-stuffs, the tongue pumping water through finely spaced lamel-lae (transverse tooth-like or comb-like ridges inside the cutting edge of the bill). Dabbling ducks suck up muddy water through the tip of the beak and squeeze it out again at the base. This makes the familiar dabbling or chattering sound as food parti-cles are filtered through water. Ducks forage for an enormous variety of food, both vegetable (including grass seeds and grains, water lilies, pond weeds, muskgrass, wigeongrass, eel-grass, wild celery, lettuce, alfalfa, windrows of kelp, plankton, algae, rice, bulbs, leaf shoots, buds, rushes, fruits or seeds of plants such as acorns, grapes, roses, rhododendrons and pines) and animal (molluscs, insects, snails, worms, limpets, crabs and crustaceans, aquatic invertebrates, small fish and fish spawn, frogs). As the folk rhyme goes: 'as Mr Frog was crossing the brook/Heigho! Said Rowley/A lily-white duck came and gobbled him up'.[11]

Ducks can dive and sift food from the mud and debris on ponds, rivers, lagoons, reservoirs and pools, pans and dams or lake bottoms, graze for seeds in fields and marshes, and sieve or filter-feed weeds and seaweeds in swamps, creeks or seas. The tribe *Tachyerini* (steamer ducks) has four species, two essentially flightless (e.g. *Tachyeres pteneres*). Their large feet enable them to swim at speed (15 knots), resembling old-fashioned paddle-steamers. Darwin described a steamer duck on his *Beagle* expedition, and his specimen can still be found in the Natural History Museum Collection at Tring. His notes include a description of the duck 'steaming' over the water with flapping wings rather than taking flight; because of the churning move-ment, Darwin thought the duck moved its wings alternately, but in fact they move simultaneously, like those of any bird.

In Rudolf Raspe's *Adventures of Baron Munchausen*, morsels of bacon on a string passed through the ducks that fly the baron home are 'strung together, like pearls on a neck-lace'.

Steamer ducks are the greedy duck heavyweights. Captain Cook, one of the first Europeans to spot them, reported weights of over 13 kg (28 lb), crammed to the gullet with shrimp and mussels.

MIGRATION

Ducks are either completely or partially migratory. The vast majority wander over wide areas in response to changing water levels. Wandering whistling ducks are nomadic and travel thousands of miles in flocks of hundreds or thousands, even hundreds of thousands in places like Sri Lanka, where they have to migrate in enormous numbers dictated by dry season changes in water supplies. The tribe *Aythyini*, freshwater diving ducks with fifteen species including ferruginous ducks (*Aythya nyroca*) and pochard, winter in India, the Mediterranean and the Sahel zone of West Africa, or the Nile Valley, and breed in Kashmir, Tibet and Siberia. In winter immense flocks of pochard visit Algerian lakes, Venetian lagoons and Indian jheels. Sightings of Baer's pochard (*Aythya baeri*) have severely declined in China and Korea, suggesting changes in migration routes to adapt for drought and loss of wetlands. The pink-headed Madagascar pochard (*Aythya innotata)* is now apparently extinct.

Many ducks are gregarious flyers and fly in groups: suddenly taking off as if by prearranged agreement in 'springs' of twenty or more at a time. Pochard, because of their short, curved wings ideal for swimming underwater, have to flap vigorously with faster wing-beats than most ducks. Light as they are (1 kg/2 lb), they can run along the water's surface for a distance before take-off, yet are known for their strong, fast flight; in fact the collective noun for a flight of pochard is a 'rush'.

Considering its hefty body weight, a mallard can fly to incredible heights.

Though they normally fly at about 150 metres (below 500 ft), ducks may fly at very high altitudes during migration (possibly to avoid dehydration) and at high speeds. A commercial airliner famously struck a mallard 7 km (4 miles) up above the Nevada desert, and ducks have been known to reach speeds of 80 kmh (50 mph) in still air, and even faster in a tail wind (or if being chased). There is only half the oxygen at this height but, flying for ten hours at a stretch, ducks can cover distances of 650–800 km (400–500 miles) a day, over incredible distances in total.

All duck flight is worth observing; it is something humans admire, perhaps because that movement is naturally denied to us, but also because of its sociability and its evident patterning, forming recognizable shapes like letters against the sky. Collective (covey) flying works like this: a duck sets off and makes way for two others, followed by another pair, whose energy inspires a fourth pair to join, and so on, until the ducks fly in an elegant 'v' formation. There are thought to be two good reasons for the v: first, the shape of formation reduces the drag

Nothern pintails (*Anas acuta*) in the air, demonstrating a gentle arc formation for communication in flight.

force each bird experiences (due to wing-tip vortices). The birds change places to spread the most fatiguing positions, with each duck at some time flying at the both the head of the v and at its tail. Second, the v-shape also allows birds to keep good visual contact and communicate easily with one another in flight.

NAVIGATION

In 1680 the astronomer Johannes Hevelius saw a constellation and group of stars to the north of Sagittarius, more or less in the centre of our galaxy. He named it 'L'Écu de Sobieski' (the crown of Sobieski) in honour of the king of Poland. This cluster of about 200 stars in the constellation 'Sobieski' is thought to look like a flock of wild duck on the wing, hence its more familiar name 'Canard Sauvage'.

Though essentially superb flyers, ducks sometimes encounter problems when flying with strong tail winds, crashing into trees or, more typically, landing with the wind at their backs, coming down with heavy splashes, overturning or sliding across the ice on their tails. In unstable air conditions the body may turn and twist, and the feet may splay wide out, but the head holds its position steadily with the horizon, as if the neck were the pivot on which everything depended. Even if you blindfold a duck and turn the body upside down, the head remains constantly oriented to gravity. Experiments with blindfolding birds and observing their hooded flight patterns have shown that ducks do not fly in circles or spirals but climb high and quickly disappear out of sight. From this we can conclude that the fact the duck cannot see probably bothers them less than it bothers the watching human scientists (who have now lost a duck *and* a blindfold). This supports the theory that skilled flyers use many other factors besides sight for navigation.

Strange images on radar called 'angels' since the 1940s are now known to be migrating birds.

How do ducks travel so far? How do they navigate? These days ducks are studied using digital video technology and radio telemetry (radio tags) to map 'site fidelity' and regular feeding grounds, distances travelled and so on. While flying, ducks use the forces of gravity and the earth's magnetic field. Bundles of magnetite have been found in the brains of birds who are thought to have a magnetic sense for the direction where the magnetic field dips most sharply – always north in the northern hemisphere – so any changes to the earth's electromagnetic

Splaying feathers for take-off, this male mallard is angled to the water but always level-headed.

properties will confuse migration routes. It is possible ducks can use sound-wave patterns (hearing super-low frequency sounds and calling continuously as they fly to listen for the sound reflected from waves and other surfaces), learn established routes and landmarks, use the horizon, the seasons, elements of weather, light and shadow, the moon and sun cycle, the solar system (reading star patterns for direction), and through a combination of known methods and multiple back-up systems, teach the young by training them in flight with the more experienced.

One unusual, important feature of the natural history of water and wildfowl is the manner in which they moult their plumage. Most other families of birds undergo a gradual moult during which the flight feathers are shed and replaced over a protracted period. Duck, on the other hand, shed all their wing feathers simultaneously, with the result that they become flightless for several weeks. The susceptibility of some male duck to predation during this flightless period is reduced by the fact that they typically moult out of their distinctive breeding colours and assume a drab appearance similar to the females and juveniles of their species. The feathering of wildfowl has other important characteristics particularly suited to the birds' aquatic lifestyles. Duck have evolved a covering of heat-retaining down beneath an outer coat of closely interlocking feathers. A gland at the base of the bird's tail secretes waterproofing oil and frequent preening serves both to distribute this oil throughout the plumage and to maintain the interlock of the feathers. Additional protection against heat loss is provided by a subcutaneous layer of fat.

Ducks often migrate without stopping to eat or drink, using their high fat reserves to manage epic journeys and weather the extreme cold and conditions of some wintering grounds.

A pet eider, or 'Cuddy's duck', at St Cuthbert's feet in the 19th-century stained-glass window in the church at Great Salkeld, Cumbria.

The famously well-feathered eider duck or Cuddy's duck[12] (*Somateriini*, four species) migrate hugging the Arctic coast in long diagonal lines and gathering in polynyas (ice pools). According to the fieldwork of Thompson and Person in 1963, probably a million eiders cross Point Barrow, Alaska, in late summer during this migration.[13] The males begin to flock early in the summer, leaving the females to form a regular migration to a safe moulting place in the sea. Breeding plumage (a v-shaped mark and green patches of colour on the sides of the head, grey or white contour feathers on mantle, breast and chin, black feathers on sides and flanks with darker coverts) goes into eclipse by July or August, losing wing (flight) feathers by late August or September. This adaptation allows the males plenty of time to make their tremendous journeys back from breeding grounds just at the moment when most other species of duck are in full moult. Were it not for such provision many

Flock of spectacled eider. Prior to 1995, no one knew where this species wintered. Satellite radio transmitters revealed them to be in the Bering Sea.

would be caught in the ice and starve before they could reach open water. In 1995 satellite radios implanted in eider pinpointed over 360,000 birds (incredibly, the entire world population) mass wintering in a unique zone of rich sub-sea molluscs in open ice leads. Massive numbers in eider flocks help keep sections of open water from freezing, and their movements help indicate the effects of global warming and climate change.

NESTING

Nesting is a variable business for ducks, depending on the context. The African white-backed duck (*Thalassornis leuconotus*), architect of the species, builds baskets of woven grasses in reeds or papyrus beds, often on fairly deep water, with a ramp leading to the nest, concealed from above by overhanging reeds. There may also be an approach channel between the nest and open water. There is an instance of a pair of muscovy duck (*Cairina moschata*) building in the steeple of a church in Sussex 24 metres (90 ft) from the ground, among the bells.

Most ducks will nest almost anywhere, on stretches of shore-line, small islets surrounded by water, nests placed in grass, dry kelp, 'diddle-dee' (empetrum), tussock grass (poa) or in reed beds, tall grass cover near water, rushes or sedges, rice fields, bush cover, old antbear, porcupine or penguin burrows, in rabbit holes, in rock or stone crevices, the hollows or holes of trees, on the slope of a ridge or hill, on sandbars or muddy flats, in clay banks, depressions in dry or wet ground, in hay or straw stacks, among driftwood, flotsam and jetsam and piles of rubbish.

Some ducks 'dump-lay' their eggs in strangers' nests, such as those of gulls or even birds of prey, and move on. An incredible 87 eggs have been counted in a single nest. More usually, ducks have their own nests, and between 2 (musk duck) and 22 (mallard) eggs are laid at a rate of one a day, female ducks pluck nest down from their underparts to complete the lining. The eggs are usually pale and unmarked, with sizes varying from 2 to 20 gm (0.07 to 0.7 oz). If a sitter is frightened away from the nest, she may release foul-smelling, oily, green excrement over her eggs before leaving, to repel predators.

Ducklings are among the best adapted of all waterfowl young, because their mother's undercarriage immediately greases their plumage so she can lead the brood straight to water a few hours after their hatching, where the liquid rolls off their downy feathers 'like water off a duck's back'. In Sergei Prokofiev's 1936 composition *Peter and the Wolf*, the little bird looked down at the duck: 'What kind of bird are you if you can't fly?' said he. To this the duck replied: 'What kind of bird are you if you can't swim?' and dived into the pond.

For the tribe *Cairinini*, thirteen species of perching and cavity nesting ducks such as mandarin (*Aix galericulata*) and wood

Wood nest-boxes can be a secure habitat for successful duck breeding.

duck (*Aix sponsa*), leaving the nest site is difficult for the young because of the drop involved, but ducklings are light, their bones soft and pliable, allowing them to fall without harm. In 1850 Thomas Bell watched a female muscovy push her newly hatched young off a beam in a barn 12 metres (40 ft) from the floor and said that they landed uninjured. Bell recorded another interesting incident, seen elsewhere in ducks:

> One day after feeding and bathing and before returning to sit on the nest, this female carefully passed the point of her bill over every egg. Then she singled one of them out, removed it about 3 yards, broke it by a stroke of her bill and returned to her duties of incubation, perfectly contented. The egg proved to be addled.[14]

Moffat's 1970 field study in Argentina described a torrent duck nest in a cliff crevice high above water from which 'he watched the ducklings drop from their cliff-side nest to the rocks 18 metres (60 ft) below at the call of their mother'.

Ducklings feed independently from their first day with the adult warming and protecting offspring, tending the youngsters until they can fly (40–70 days, according to species). The young of most duck species are sexually mature by 9–11 months, so they breed in the second summer of their life. The duration of a pair bond varies; in most species of duck it is short and ends with egg-laying, males having little or nothing to do with incubation, while in others the males remain near the females until the young hatch, then gather into large flocks of males.

GATHERING AND SOCIABILITY

Though the social highlight of the tribe *Dendrocygnini* (eight species of whistling or tree duck) is the fulvous duck's (*Dendrocygna bicolor*) famous long-legged, post-copulatory 'step-dance' (in which the pair display unusually on land rather than water), Red-bills' (*Dendrocygna autumnalis*) communal roosting, sharing large clutches of eggs in dump nests and carrying the young on their backs, has led many breeders to believe that gathering and social interaction is the key to whistling ducks' productivity. The 'new men' of ducks, *Dendrocygnini* males participate actively with incubation, sit and guard the nest, do not quarrel and are very gentle and familiar in their habits. They have a curious habit of mixing with and caring for strange young birds of other species, defending them against enemies.

Silent in aviaries, *Dendrocygnini* are vocal on the wing, flying in irregular formations, preening each other and gathering in huge flocks in the wild. Though, in 1857, 'veritable clouds' were seen in the Sudan,[15] the fact that they are – somewhat fatally – unwary, slow fliers, suggested these numbers might not last. Among the most cosmopolitan of all birds, they breed in North

Fulvous whistling duck (*Dendrocygna bicolor*), whose under-wing feathers look like Impressionist sweeps of paint, and striking, almost tortoise-shell plumage of warm russet tones shown to great advantage in late afternoon light.

and South America, Africa and Asia in a variety of habitats from lowlands to an astonishing 3.35 km (11,000 ft) up.[16]

Most waterfowl are very sociable when not nesting. Some winter gatherings can be enormous, such as wintering flocks of Baikal teal (*Anas formosa*) in Japan, where 100,000 have been seen near Osaka. King eider (*Somateria spectabilis*) form crèches of a hundred or more ducklings, shared by a few females. The other females and males migrate in vast flocks to moulting areas at sea, a thousand miles away from the nest.

In captivity tree ducks such as lesser or Indian whistling teal (*Dendrocygna javanica*) become exceedingly tame; it is possible to keep them in complete freedom without their making any attempt to leave the home pond; they feed from the hand, habitually whistle in reply when called, become rather inactive and reach advanced years. In 1883 the London Zoological

Gardens had four specimens of black-billed or Cuban whistling duck (*Dendrocygna arborea*) that had lived there for the past twenty years.

DISPLAY

One of the most notable aspects of human interpretation of waterfowl behaviour is response to duck ritual displays. Duck sexual behaviour interests humans greatly, down to the last possible detail. Ducks breed following various courtship or pair-maintaining displays, sometimes involving intense competition among males with breast-to-breast fighting and aerial chasing (both male and female birds, though mostly males, have been observed in courtship flights, plumage change, shaking, tail cocking, head, chin or tail lifting, 'nod-swimming', burp or grunt-whistling, head or bill-dipping – often called 'false drinking' – raising a 'sail' feather or wings and calling) and mutual head-pumping (repetitive bobbing of the head up and down). The tribe comprising eight species of *Oxyurini* (stiff-tailed ducks) have long stiffened shafts of tail feathers that serve as underwater rudders and display features, plus large feet placed so far back it is difficult to walk on land. The endangered white-headed duck (*Oxyura leucocephala*) rarely flies and makes

A sketch of display behaviour, including swimming with outstretched neck or 'ritual drinking'.

Mutual chin-lifting of a pair of Chiloe wigeon.

almost no vocal sounds, but like the ruddy duck (*Oxyura jamaicensis*) can contort their necks and tails into striking postures for communication and display.

In 1898 Phillips saw the whole of the vast sound of Currituck in North Carolina as 'paved with Ruddies. I can only describe it by saying it looked as if one could walk dry-shod . . . some eight miles, without getting his feet wet, by simply stepping on the backs of these ducks!'[17] The enormous number of fond vernacular names given to this species (such as booby duck, bumble-bee coot, sleepy-head, fool duck, deaf duck, dumpling duck, shot-pouch and horse-turd dipper) points to how easy it is to catch or shoot. The ruddy duck also has an allegedly 'ludicrous courtship performance' like a puppet pulled by strings, lifting his tail up and down, tapping his chest with his bill (a large air-sac opening at the windpipe used as a sounding board during display), drumming out a croaking 'tick-tick-tick-tickety-quek' and 'boiling' the water with wings and feet. Females commonly mimic males in display postures. Whitehead's observations of *Oxyurini* in 1885 demonstrate a recurrent tendency for analogies to human behaviour, since he describes how they hoist their tails up, 'spreading every feather to the utmost, like a hand with all the fingers spread out', and Phillips wryly observes: 'I

Ruddy duck in display position, stiffened tail held high.

Duck feeding, tail up, having thrown up a shower of spray.

daresay this ruddy is fully as slipshod in its maternal affairs as we are.'[18]

As with human species, stories of rape and pillage have shaped duck history, and like human behaviour on the Costa del Sol and elsewhere around the world, sexual tourism remains a controversial subject. The UK ruddy duck population, descended from a few birds imported by the Wildfowl Trust after the Second World War, settled at Slimbridge Bird

The endangered white-headed duck.

Sanctuary, but did not stay put, and this is where the trouble began. 'The best known member of the stiff-tailed group is the aptly named ruddy duck, as in Britain this charming and entertaining stiff-tail is proving itself to be a ruddy nuisance, due to its tendency to wander off to Spain and seduce white-headed ducks.'[19] In the early 1990s the ruddy duck fell from grace when Spanish ornithologists reported that invading male ruddy ducks had arrived on lakes in Andalusia inhabited by the rare, endangered white-headed duck, a closely related stiff-tail. The aggressive ruddies were

> seducing, even raping the female white-headed ducks, and hybrids were appearing as a result. As the Spanish had spent a good deal of time, money and effort on restoring the white-headed duck population, they were not too pleased. An urgent report was sent to Britain, asking that the ruddy ducks should be controlled and thus stopped from heading for Spain, and indulging in such lager-lout behaviour. This threw the British ornithological hierarchy into turmoil.[20]

English Nature, the RSPB and the Wildfowl and Wetlands Trusts agreed that control was needed. Many ruddy duck have since been shot and had their nests destroyed, but by the late 1990s they were nesting again in France and the Netherlands . . .

Though courtship is a term used to include the whole sequence of events in the pairing of sexes, it is notable that display does not always lead to copulation, as the male musk duck (*Biziura lobata*) from Australia and Tasmania shows:

> This display – perhaps the most dramatic of all birds – draws both males and females, who crowd round the

38

courting male. Often males become more attracted than females, swimming much closer to the displaying male and sometimes even making physical contact by gently and repeatedly nudging their beaks against his shoulder. The displaying male is in a trance-like state and rarely responds directly to any of the onlookers.[21]

According to Johnsgard, the musk duck is unusual in that when females approach displaying males, they 'suddenly attempt to copulate in a rape-like manner. Seemingly no association between the pairs occurs . . . There appears to be a greater development of promiscuous mating systems than in perhaps any other species of this family.'[22]

SEX LIVES

In Greek mythology, *Anas platyrhynchos* (mallard) were connected with the cult of *Aphrodite* (goddess of love and hunter/warrior) and consequently with Eros. In Rethymno museum, Crete, a sculpture of Aphrodite from Ancient Lappa has the goddess resting a foot lightly on the back of a duck. It has been suggested that Aphrodite was originally an Asian fertility goddess whose domain embraced all nature – vegetable and animal – as well as human (just as ducks do).

The British tabloid press often features 'amorous' duck stories, such as 'Lovelorn Jake's 8-mile duck walk' in 2005, when a muscovy duck who had been removed from a country park because of his rape behaviours then walked 12 km (7.5 miles) back across north Devon without, according to a wildfowl specialist, 'any natural homing instinct whatever'. In the same spring, another article from a London newspaper carried a story about single ducks in London's royal parks 'looking for a partner' to encourage breeding. 'With Valentine's Day in mind, the royal parks are urging the public to sponsor a duck to help fund "Operation Love a Duck" . . . Sponsors will receive a photograph, a certificate and the chance to name and keep track of their duck.'[23] Human double standards: either duck decide entirely for themselves or we for them; understood in terms of love and romance rather than sex and mating.

Typically, duck such as mallard will display, then copulate or 'tread' in water of swimming depth. Though most birds copulate without a penis, McCracken's study of *Oxyura vittata* (Argentine lake duck or blue-bill) in 2000 revealed a long 'ornamented' penis half the duck's body length with an 'array of dense spines running the length of the organ and a thorny, brush-like texture'. Having first measured the organ at 20 cm, McCracken and colleagues found a specimen a year later with a penis nearly half a metre long.[24] The fact that this organ is uncommon in birds but present in non-avian groups such as crocodiles and turtles suggests that a well-developed penis in many dabbling and diving ducks may derive from copulating in water. After treading, either or both sex can rise in the water, wing-flap and call, while each vertically raises its wing on the side opposite its partner, or the partner raises the other's wing with its beak. They often turn to face their heads to one another for a few seconds, followed by a post-copulative display, where they bathe or preen themselves or one another. Hudson first described, in 1876, mallards' nuptial flights where 'every time they came close they slap each other on the wings so smartly the sound can be distinctly heard, like applauding hand-claps'.[25] In 1907 Crawshay recorded 'a merry tourney on the water' followed by 'a reckless dashing flight-wheeling, twisting, doubling, stooping and rising'.[26]

The male
Argentine Lake
duck and his
42.5 cm penis.

   The courtship behaviour of the Chiloe wigeon (*Anas sibilatrix*) was compared by Konrad Lorenz in the early 1950s to an anserine triumph ceremony, interpreted as the species' strong pair bond. This has since been discovered to be more diverse, since in the wild it is not probable that a pair will stay together

Mutual preening is part of post-copulative duck behaviour.

for more than one season (January to May) or likely that attachments are permanent ones. In China and Japan the mandarin duck (*Aix galericulata*) still symbolizes happiness and marital fidelity, yet studies have long revealed that mandarin ducks force copulate and their population is dwindling, suggesting poor attachment patterns. The myth that ducks (like swans) are permanently pair-forming, monogamous birds is refuted by observation in the field, where many male birds make attempted rape chases, and their possible role in normal pair formation is dubious. In fact, some ducks' sexual behaviour can be positively deviant.

Forced copulation or mating, less sociologically charged terms for rape (copulation without consent, resisted to the best of the victim's ability), is thought highly unusual in the animal world, but has been studied in ducks, geese and insects such as the damselfly. Sexual coercion typically occurs in the animal world where the male (or female) has the strength or a specific organ designed to restrain during copulation (such as the male scorpion-fly), but research into 'convenience polyandry' (accepting more than one mate at a time) suggests that the relative safety of submitting to some forced mating may reduce the

春水初生漲碧池眠流何以散相思含情
欲問鴛鴦鳥漠對桃花題一詩
戊辰長朝新霏文宿士歌圖圖

A happy couple is called a 'mandarin duck couple' in China and Japan, where the birds are symbols of love and fidelity.

Due to the risks to the female with mating or 'treading' in the water, female ducks can drown.

risks of repeated harassment, wounding or death. When artificially crowded, males can become exceedingly troublesome. Huxley, observing an incredible 1,200 pairs breeding on Tring reservoir in 1912, recorded 70 females killed by drowning that year by forced copulation.[27] Grandin and Johnson have argued that over-selection inevitably results in neurological damage resulting in further unnatural practices, such as intensive breeders' need for 'debeaking' or bill trimming to avoid females' attacks on penises in overcrowded factory farm conditions.[28]

As many as 40 males may chase a single female in aerial or aquatic pursuit; drakes have been known to grab and mount females underwater when they dive (attempting escape) or knock females to the ground in mid-flight. In some populations as many as 7–10 per cent of all females die each year as a result of drowning or injuries incurred during rapes. In March 2005 *The Register* ran an article titled 'Boffin Honoured for Necrophile Gay Duck Paper', detailing the work of researcher Kees Moelikers, an 'Ig Nobel' prizewinner, for his improbable findings on homosexual necrophilia in *Anas platyrhynchos*.[29] Bruce Bagemihl concurs:

> Occasionally, males even mate with dead males. While they are still paired in the mating season, males frequently court and attempt to mate with (or rape) females other than their mate. About 3–7% of offspring are a result of such non-monogamous mating, and in some populations multiple parentage occurs in at least 17–25% of broods.[30]

The tribe *Anatini* (dabbling ducks) demonstrates all the homosexual and bisexual non-reproductive, promiscuous behaviours that Bagemihl's study of animal homosexuality points to: pair bonds with same-sex partners, courting, mounting and copulating out of the breeding season, including forcibly. Mallard pairs commonly separate, or 'divorce' as some ornithologists put it, and single or groups of females raise families without males, share or exchange nests, and adopt extra ducklings.

Anatini, with about 40 species, is the most common duck in the world; the duck with the recognizable 'quack'. The Latin

Single-sex mallard pairs can often be observed demonstrating courtship and mating behaviours.

name for mallard was originally *Anas boschas*, and it is invariably 'wild duck' in any vernacular, from *wilde Ente, canard sauvage, pato real*, to the Turkish *ordek* or Mongolian *azin*: simply 'duck'. Most breeds of domestic duck derive from the mallard: toy mallard call ducks, the Rouen giant mallard, the Pekin, Aylesbury ducks, the Penguin and Indian runner ducks. Staying fertile, *Anatini* hybridize readily with other species and also show extraordinary diversity within its own tribe. They are hunted, painted and kept by humans, from gadwall (*Anas strepera*) in the marshes, to teal (blue-winged, *Anas discors*) on the wing; from 'spoonbills' (northern shoveller, *Anas clypeata*) as the most outwardly distinctive to European widgeon (*Anas Penelope*) 'of lovely shape' like Penelope, the ever faithful and devoted wife of Homer's Odysseus. *Anatini* increasingly assimilates other tribes into itself (such as *Cairinini* and *Stictonettini*). The most well known of the dabbling ducks, mallard (*Anas platyrhynchos* or 'flat nose') are undoubtedly the most abundant in the world. Perhaps it is their adaptability, not least in terms of flexible sexuality and the ability to live both wild and tame, that makes them one of the most familiar tribes to humans.

A green-winged teal drake, part of a common species.

Northern pintail (*Anas acuta*).

Northern shoveller, shovel-shaped bill in profile, plus the full variation of plumage with strong primary and secondary flight feathers.

2 The Free and the Pressed

Of the species of wildfowl in the world, the 'edible' are defined in Western texts as mallard, teal, pintail, shoveller and gadwall, the 'non-edible' are scoters, scaup, golden-eye and long- or stiff-tailed ducks.[1] In the US and Canada a huge abundance of ducks, public right of way over land and the right to own a gun make hunting easy. When Charles Dickens visited the US in 1842 he wrote of wide streams blackened by flocks of wild ducks. These would have been canvasback ducks, the tastiest of America's indigenous breeds. By the mid-nineteenth century professional hunting of swans, geese and duck on a vast scale depleted wild-fowl so rapidly that public concern resulted in US Congress passing the Migratory Bird Act in 1918 to put an end to market hunting. Hunting on an individual basis continues to this day, and shows no signs of declining.

Duck hunting has been a traditional way to catch game to eat for the last 8,000 years, as well as a popular sport. It is said to be relaxing, anticipatory, offering the companionship of dogs and other humans with the chance to feel at one with nature in the dark, dusk and dawn. Yet the first motives were hunger and need; subsistence hunting is as much a feature of poorer regions as game sports as leisure activities are of the richer. The

Pisanello, *Two Teal*, 1430s, ink drawing with watercolour and wash.

typology of animal exploitation has revised the subsistence systems of hunting, herding and agriculture long held to be sequential into a new sequence: 'predation' (hunting for protein), 'protection' (free-range herding and taming of pets) and 'domestication' (breeding in isolation from the wild). Though the Siriono of Bolivia and Waimiri Atroari Indians of Brazil were still subsistence hunting whistling duck and muscovy in 2000, duck hunting in the West has moved from a subsistence activity to a social game, a luxury rather than a necessity, with two emerging trends: recreational and specialist hunting. While the initial economic importance of hunting steadily

The Federal Duck
or Migratory Bird
Hunting and
Conservation
Stamp for 2005.

decreased and hunting tourism became the new variation, the demands for high levels of sport harvest brought controversy over duck hunting regulations.

In 1934 the Migratory Bird Hunting Stamp Act (or 'Duck Stamp Act') was passed by US Congress, requiring the purchase of a Federal Duck Stamp by waterfowl hunters to generate revenue to protect wetlands. Since its inception, it is thought that the programme has protected 4.5 million acres of waterfowl habitat. Duck hunters in North America and elsewhere take pains to ensure the continuity of their sport by funding wetlands conservation. The private organization Ducks Unlimited has over a million supporters. Founded by duck hunters in 1937, it has concentrated on saving the main wildfowl-nesting habitats in North America, in particular the 906,500 square km (350,000 sq. mile) wetlands of the Canadian and US prairies called the 'duck factory'. It has done this by raising money to buy swamps, attaching entails to prevent drainage and selling the swamps on. It has paid farmers the market rate not to drain them. The ducks do well, with species increasing, it is argued, while wildlife hunters and photographers benefit because they want to shoot more ducks.

The struggle between farmers, hunters and governments goes on, however, with national subsidies affecting 'developing' country farmers and duck habitat on an international scale, plus pressure from the anti-hunting fraternity from the big cities, who want to turn wetlands into theme parks for city dwellers. Yet this theme – of townies as the root of all misunderstanding and damage to 'countryside traditions' – is by now a tired cliché. As progress makes demands on both city and countryside life, it increasingly exposes the contradictions and the interrelatedness of hunting and conservation. Banding or bird-ringing, fitting numbered light metal rings

Ornithologist ringing (banding) a duck in Saskatchewan, Canada, in the early 1950s.

to bird necks or legs for large-scale research, began in 1898 when a red-breasted merganser (*Mergus serrator*) was marked by H.C.C. Mortensen of Denmark, the first ornithologist to mark birds extensively for science. It has defined over four continental flyways, and organizations such as Ducks Unlimited juggle the conflicting or complementary interests of hunting, conservation and waterfowl management. Specialist hunters have been characterized as either 'enthusiasts' (amateurs who hunt large numbers and do most damage) or 'participants' (older, experienced waterfowl hunters who hunt small numbers and are aware of the need for 'refuges' for migratory waterfowl, since over-hunting disturbs and displaces the birds significantly). Refuge creation is working to improve conservation value and the biodiversity of wetlands of most importance to waterfowl, and forecasts include a larger role for women as professional wildlife managers and hunters, taking a more holistic view of wetland management.[2] Women hunters represent 1 per cent of the US population and 9 per cent of all hunters, according to a 2001 survey of fishing, hunting and wildlife-associated recreation.

Three types of duck netting: concealed in trees, in the open and on water (from Diderot's *Encyclopédie*, 1751–72).

Though duck hunting these days conjures up the image of a gun, in fact weapons for duck hunting and killing have included bare hands, missiles, stones, darts, spears, blow pipes, arrows, pellets, hawks or falcons, drugs, snares, traps, funnels, baited hooks, bird lime and nets. Netting birds is an immemorial practice: 5,000 years ago the Ice Man recently found frozen in the Alps carried a bird net identical to those used in Portugal today. Ornamental depictions of Chinese emperors show them hunting with bow and arrow, showing off their skill on horseback chasing flying duck. Aztec manuscripts show hunters with all their weapons and individual characteristics, including the association of each to a bird. The Zsujta duck of 1200–1050 BC was found with a hoard of weapons.

'Waterfowl shall come to you in their thousands', reads an Egyptian coffin text. Egyptians used large hexagonal nets to catch

Egyptian waterfowling scene: a fragment of wall painting from a tomb of c. 1350 BC.

A Hidatsa Indian called 'White Duck', posed wearing a head-dress of duck-down, skin and feathers, c. 1908.

enormous numbers of migratory birds, putting decoys in the water or flushing the ducks out of their hiding places with dogs or civets. 'You have cast your throw-stick at them and a thousand have been felled', continues the text.[3] Where Egyptians used throw sticks, ancient Eskimo and Amarind peoples hunted with bow and arrow and other cleverly devised tools to throw into flocks of duck. Bolas weapons – ivory weights attached by hide and braided sinew thongs, bound together at a bone handle with a bundle of bird quills and sedge – are known to have featured in the Birnirk culture of north-western Alaska. Alaskan native peoples were ready to trade iron and tobacco for furs and artefacts, which found their way into nineteenth-century museum collections.[4] Eskimos hunted widely with bolas: in the hunting season men and women wore them wound round their heads, to be thrown at a moment's notice when hunting birds on land and, adapted with driftwood weights, for sea hunts. The Alaska bird spear – made of wood, bone and sinew – was thrown from a kayak using a throwing board (*atatl*) to increase the speed of the spear, skimming over the water to catch waterfowl by the neck or wing during the summer moult when they could not fly.

The early peoples of North America also hunted duck, with some duck traditions – such as dances – lasting to this day. The ritual forms part of the *hesi* cycle (imitative dances) of the Patwin and Maidu of California, while the Kutchin waddle and wave their arms like ducks to ensure a good catch out hunting; the Iroquois cry 'Hat-Hat', and the men are joined by impersonations of the spirits of plenty, to encourage duck multiplication.[5] But for catching duck, decoys are needed, and their history is as old as hunting itself. Without duck decoys, a duck hunt would usually involve employing beaters to scare the birds into flight out of the wetlands, so they could be netted or shot. Every year since 1279 a great duck hunt was held on the *étangs* (ponds) of Ponthieu in France. Many local peasants were obliged to assist in driving the birds, even stripping off and entering the water to drive the ducks out of the reed beds. Great bag nets (*panneaux*) were extended at regular intervals along the lake, though mass netting provoked conservation legislation from the 1500s onwards.

HUNTING BY DECOY

The word 'decoy' means two things: a fake or a trap. There are two kinds of duck decoys: one a large netted construction to trap a number of birds, the other a fake duck used to trap a real duck.

The first type of engineered decoy is almost certainly a Dutch innovation: the word comes either from the Dutch *de Kooi* (cage or trap) or *eendekooy/eende kooi* (duck cage), from this ingenious method of harvesting wildfowl used in the Netherlands from the seventeenth century. This kind of decoy is composed of a number of 'pipes' narrowing to tunnels with a 'purse' at the end, covered by netted hoops made of wych elm,

The Boarstall Duck Decoy, Bucking-hamshire, in the 1890s.

willow, ash or metal, which radiate from a pond or lake surrounded by woodland. Ducks are tempted by grain, potatoes or the quacking of live decoys to enter, then a *kooikerhondje* (little cage dog) or 'piper' dog and decoyman would drive the ducks to their fate. As early as 1432, 600 wildfowl were recorded as having been stolen out of the Abbot's Decoys at Crowland Abbey, Norfolk, but decoys are formally recorded as introduced into Britain by Dutch drainage engineers employed to drain the great marshes in the East Anglian Fens around 1650. Similar decoys existed in other parts of Britain: St James's Park in London had a 'King's Decoy' established by Charles II around 1665 as a source of duck for the table, built for him by a Dutchman variously named Hydrach Hilens or Sydrach Hilcus. There is also a fine example in working order in Buckinghamshire, the Boarstall Duck Decoy, constructed between 1691 and 1697.

The Dutch had their decoys in the Wadden sea region, especially the western side of the Lauwers Zee in Friesland, where

56

widgeon and teal gathered in thousands. Pond decoys were extremely popular in Britain, the Netherlands, France and Germany from the seventeenth century to the early twentieth. There were over 200 in Britain by the end of the nineteenth century; some in East Anglia were recording catches of over 5,000 ducks per season. By 1918 there were only 28 remaining, and the slaughter of ducks on this scale by this method had ceased in Britain by 1954. In 1980, when the National Trust acquired Boarstall, only three or four decoys were left working in the country and Boarstall was one of two that still used a piper dog. Wildfowl are caught in decoys like Boarstall now only for

A hunter sets duck decoys in the sunlight.

Gentlemen and dogs pursue a mallard in *Duck-baiting*, an 1820s print by Henry Thomas Alken.

scientific purposes: to be ringed, recorded and released again. Decoys are restored or maintained as country heritage sites open to the general public and nature reserves (where ducks now enjoy respite from the attentions of fowlers).

The second kind of decoy is an established folk art in the US, Canada and Europe, and hand-carved and painted wooden ducks from well-known decoy-makers are sought-after antiques.[6] An Elmer Crowell decoy (a Massachusetts carver, 1862–1951) fetched $684,500 at a Sotheby's sale, the highest-flying sale price to date. It is clear that humans fall for decoys. So do ducks, but why? So strong, it is generally agreed, are the drives to eat and gather sociably that a duck will risk much to go wherever it thinks other ducks are. Decoys are often used with a 'blind' or a 'sink box' (a boat, hidden among the reeds, sunk into the water), a fixed shelter, a 'grave' (a shallow trench dug in a stubble field) or a 'hide' (any place to stalk a stretch of water) to conceal the hunters.

Crafted decoys can be fold-up silhouette or shadow birds made of card, solid birds made from grasses or reeds, cork, plastic or wood or inflatable rubber, or stuffed dead birds. In 1911, during the mining of bat guano for fertilizer in a cave 22 miles south-west of Lovelock in the Humbult valley in west-central Nevada, a remarkable find was made: numerous well-preserved Native American objects, amongst them eleven canvas-back decoys, over 1,000 years old. These were made of tule rush reeds bound together in duck shape and covered with the skin and feathers of the bird to add realism. Other finds included bird bones elaborately ornamented with incised designs and whistles for bird hunting. Legend and local folklore suggest that the cave was used as a trap for killing an entire rival tribe in competition for food (the seeds and waterfowl of the nearby lakes).[7]

Hunting was often done with birds of prey or dogs. Though the first duck-droving (herding) dog was a poodle, preferred gun dogs are self-restrained ones with soft mouths that will not damage the bird, such as retrievers, labradors and spaniels. Essentially, even when hunting duck with 'duck hawks' (the peregrine falcon in the US and Arab states, the marsh harrier or moor buzzard in the UK), any hunting animal must be well trained, obedient to whistles and silent signals and reliable to 'fetch' or kill.

Lewis Clement travelled to Abbeville, near Amiens in France, in 1871 to try duck decoying in the French style, and later wrote up his experiences, as hunters still do. The Englishman was invited by the local duck decoyman (or *huttier*) to his tiny night-hut – apparently 'uncommonly like a dunghill' – which he shared with three live decoy ducks (trapped and tied together) and a wet poodle. This sets the scene for what

A successful hunt: a black retriever poses with his duck . . .

. . . as do a group of humans with theirs, including a woman hunter dressed in camouflage.

is representative of an entire oeuvre of hunting descriptions of male bonding in close (if not foetid) quarters. 'Old Pierre' explains that he has once accidentally shot his decoy drake, which ever since understandably 'ducks his head when the gun goes off'. As wild duck fly overhead, the decoy ducks 'quack' furiously, drawing them in. Clement describes this in terms of 'light-principled females' or ' unfaithful wives having a flirtation with the newcomers', which infuriates the drake:

> The two ducks, aware of his jealousy, and of the approach
> of the wild birds, continued, repeatedly, as if in defiance
> of their lawful lord and master, to call out softly, to plume
> themselves, and to duck under water, and make them-

selves altogether as pretty and interesting as circum-
stances would permit.

Human preoccupation with the duck's sexual relations takes
on the language of romantic farce: the 'flirtation' of 'unfaithful
wives', the 'jealousy' of a 'lawful lord and master'. Gun types are
as loaded with evidence of social hierarchies. In 1871 Old Pierre
used a muzzle-loader rather than a breech-loader as loyal to his
class: 'Because all the other *huttiers* would call me an *aristocrate*.'[8]

HUNTING BY GUN

There was a little man, and he had a little gun,
And his bullets were made of lead, lead, lead;
He went to the brook, and saw a little duck,
And shot it right through its little head, head, head.[9]

Between 1876 and 1878 the Russian explorer Colonel N.
Przhevalsky travelled with a party of Cossacks to the heart of
central Asia, across the Tian Shan to Lob-Nor, in Mongolia.
Przhevalsky noted a wealth of pintail ducks, pochards and gad-
walls on Lob-Nor, a massive freshwater lake once thought to be
salt. In February ducks arrived by the thousands; by March they
were gone again. 'Seated on the ice, the flocks murmured to
themselves as though taking counsel together on their further
flight northwards.' The locals had no guns, but ducks trapped in
nets were variety to the fish diet, and fully used in other respects.
Przhevalsky found inhabitants of Lob-Nor using fish and duck as
a regular part of purchase money for brides: 'Girls marry at the
age of 14 or 15 and the "kalym" or dowry is 10 bundles of cloth,
10 strings of dried fish, and 200 ducks.' 'In Winter, the cloaks are
lined with duck skins dressed with salt, whilst the down and

A 1950s tableau of punt guns against a 'duck-billed reptile' in a museum. Punt guns (huge shotguns) enabled market hunters to bring down between 30 and 100 diving ducks per shot, before they became illegal in the USA in 1918.

feathers are mixed with the dry reeds and used for bedding.' In sharp contrast, all of Przhevalsky's party of Russian Cossacks carried rifles, so

> Duck shooting was always absurdly easy. We counted the slain by dozens, although we husbanded our ammunition, having only a small quantity, and no use for half the ducks we killed. Of these we required three apiece for food, so that we boiled 24 ducks in our saucepan for breakfast, lunch and supper daily. Such are traveller's appetites sharpened by outdoor life and constant exercise – the best of antidotes against stomachic disorders and sleeplessness.[10]

The history of modern waterfowl hunting essentially parallels the evolution of the shotgun, since neither falcons nor longbows could match shot. Gun types vary enormously, from extremely elegant bespoke sports and hobby equipment to what seem to be more or less cannons. Contemporary North American and Canadian duck hunting and shooting books, anecdotes or advertisements tend to take a no-nonsense (even macho) tone: 'create a pattern of natural calm . . . then move in for the kill . . . dozens of duck will succumb to a dose of cold steel . . .'. 'If you shoot my guns: all new Benelli M1-90 autos in 12 and 20 gauge, all you need to do is get on the plane and come on down.'[11] Yet, referring back to the little ditty, in the US, UK and Canada, by law all shot used for waterfowl must now be non-toxic (lead-free).

Once a duck has been shot or wounded, some hunters leave it to die, but traditional hunting manuals recommend hand-killing quickly and mercifully:

> With both hands grasp the duck by the shoulders, belly up and with his head away from you. A small stone, a log, the edge of a blind or the bar of the boat will make a suitable anvil. Swing the duck up over your shoulder and bring the back of his head down smartly upon the anvil you have chosen . . . even if the first blow does not kill the duck it will at least render him unconscious and end his suffering. The second or third blow will end his life. It is an unpleasant proceeding, I know. But you wounded the duck, and it is up to you to finish the job humanely.[12]

Hunters are aware of the technical irony of killing by hand after shooting. The recriminatory tone above ('you wounded the duck') is one also found in retired duck hunters, who see no contradiction in moving on to duck conservation in private

Ducks in an 18th-century Mughal painting.

sanctuaries or former duck decoys. This 'payment of dues' attitude is preserved in myth. A Japanese folk tale describes how Sonjo the hunter came across a mandarin duck pair in the rushes of Lake Akanuma, killed the male, cooked and ate him.[13] That night he dreamed he saw a beautiful woman weeping bitterly. She reproached Sonjo for killing her husband and told him to go again to the rushes. When he did so, a female duck swam straight towards him, tore open her breast with her beak and died before his eyes. Sonjo was so shaken he gave up hunting and became a monk. This story is often performed in Japan in *kage'e* (a shadow picture) with puppets in front of a back-lit screen. At the moment of her death, the puppet of the female duck is replaced by another puppet, this time theatrically tripled in size, magnifying the weight of Sonjo's sin and the female duck's sorrow.[14]

With diverse cultural histories, many models of the hunter permeate the modern world. What seems most at issue is the hunter's (symbolic) relationship and status as a reflection of those different societies. It is argued that agricultural development led to increasingly class-divided societies and specialist functionalist categories. If the old cultures of China, Russia and Europe maintained a social order where a minority of royalty and aristocrats shot duck (and peasants who happened to get in the way), a majority across the US and Canada were proud of duck hunting as sport for 'ordinary folk'. Whom we allow the 'freedom to hunt' relates in Asia and Russia to royal histories, in Europe to class distinctions, in the US and Canada to a frontier spirit to make free with the wild, a constitutional right for every citizen.

Class is inextricably linked to duck hunting. In the era of the Mongolian empire, Marco Polo related the importance of game birds to the imperial cuisine, where Mongols obtained a large portion of their food by the chase. Imperial game also supplemented the rural population's diet. In many parts of early medieval Europe agricultural production was insufficient to feed the population and hunting still had a place in the domestic economies of noble and peasant. Hunting behaviours and clothing developed. The Miwok people of what is now California first rid themselves of their clothes and human smell in 'sweat lodges' and wore costume (such as duck masks) to take on the attributes of the animal hunted (hunting in hide and feathers to catch hide and feathers). Arctic peoples produced parkas with up to 60 stitched pieces lined with duck-down

An Eskimo adult and child wearing duck-skin parkas, Nunivak Island, Alaska, 1929.

feathers, capable of withstanding sub-zero temperatures, while other Native Americans wore tanned skin shirts and leggings for the hunt. From the sixteenth century to the nineteenth in the West, sporting gentlemen and the military wore leggings ('spatterdashes') or breeches made of woollen cloth or leather, a fashion for 'hunting shirts' associated with the frontier in North America appearing in the eighteenth century. Later, the 'shooting jacket' (a sports coat with leather patches on elbows and the front shoulder to prevent wear from the butt of the shotgun or rifle) became popular. Camouflage materials gave hunting a military look and are now commercially marketed, as are wool and silk underwear, quilted duck- and goose-down layers in 'blanket' trousers for winter hunting, hooded jackets, caps with flaps, socks, rubber and insulated boots.

Boots have always been important indicators of social status for the hunter, in terms of their quality and material. Mongols first wore the special riding boots later (by the 1870s) to be known as cowboy boots: a narrower, high-heeled version of the military design, to fit but not slip from the stirrup. Duck hunters traditionally wear leather boots since *waders will drown you*.[15] A major problem is keeping warm, hence the uses for lard, gloves made of wool and rubber, pocket warmers and a variety of tipples. In a modern post-colonial context duck-hunting images invariably depict the male hunter in camouflage or combat clothing, with gun and a string of dead ducks – more than he and his family could possibly eat. The more ducks the better in fact, since it's a competitive sport and most is best, which is the most disturbing aspect of the Przhevalsky story.

A pair of hunters wading through a swamped hardwood forest.

Mass hunting of game birds for the upper-class table and restaurant trade pushed several species to the brink of extinction during the late 1800s and early 1900s.

Though women have often been involved in hunting, they have been historically portrayed as being in such absurdly robust physical health as to slip into comic visual jokes about lesbianism. And though today women from all walks of life are being actively encouraged to participate in duck hunting, with 'Duck Hunting Clinics' and women-only hunts in American and Canadian state parks, the most familiar picture of duck hunting for the European man or woman is as an upper-class pursuit. Set in 1913, the twilight of the Edwardian era, Isabel Colegate's novel *The Shooting Party* is the story of an aristocratic game shoot on a country estate on the eve of the Great War. The adults are gathered for tea on the afternoon before the shoot when an unexpected visitor enters the room: a young female mallard in the peak of condition. The wild duck

shook its feathers slightly, then slowly extended one leg sideways as if in a dance movement. It then stretched one wing along the length of the leg, opening to view a patch of deep bright blue feathers barred with white which it had been concealing beneath the speckled brown of its wing. 'How beautiful,' said Olivia . . . The duck now with a surprisingly loud sputtering sound emitted a large damp dropping. Cicely giggled. The duck walked slowly forward and lowering its head began to dabble, or graze, at a Persian carpet.[16]

In rushes the child Osbert, to whom the duck belongs, who is warned to keep his pet inside the following day. However, on the day of the shoot, Osbert's duck has escaped among the wild duck; village beaters – many of whom will soon be called up for the trenches – are in exposed positions in the wood, and a Christian activist, declaring 'Thou Shalt Not Kill', has placed himself in the path of what he calls 'the massacre'. As the child and a servant frantically search the wetlands, the rivalry between hunters becomes so fierce that they stop 'shooting like gentlemen' and just as the pet duck is found alive, a beater is accidentally shot and dies horribly.

Osbert's duck – its beauty natural rather than 'civilized', its vulnerability heightened, a wild thing now dangerously too trusting – is not shot after all. But a human is – a lowly beater. How this corrupt society (de)values life is satirized by *The Shooting Party*, especially how the domestic is servant to a (*sauvage*/wild) uncivilized elite. It is a familiar theme. As early as 1884 Henrik Ibsen's play *The Wild Duck* used the confinement of a wounded wild duck rescued by a young woman as a metaphor for frustrated domestic life. Made on the eve of the Second World War – and promptly banned by the French government as demoralizing and unpatriotic – Jean Renoir's 1939 film comedy *La Règle du jeu* (*The Rules of the Game*) is bleak about human prospects: 'Do you like hunting?' one woman asks another, who raises a nonchalant eyebrow and shrugs no,

Gabriel Metsu, *The Sleeping Sportsman*, c. 1660s, oil on canvas.

whilst killing everything in sight. Gabriel Metsu's classic genre painting *The Sleeping Sportsman* (Wallace Collection, London) indicates more has been going on than just hunting. Behind the dead duck hanging from the tree in the foreground are a dishevelled countrywoman and sportsman; worn out from the chase in all senses. *Vogelen*, 'to bird', is Dutch slang for both bird hunting and copulating, and in the seventeenth century a knowing viewer would have made this association.[17]

But who speaks for the duck? In the contemporary West, it is cartoons and children's literature. There you will find all the humour of the unstable subject. In *Duck! Rabbit! Duck!*, a 'Merrie Melodies' cartoon of 1953, Daffy Duck removes and burns every 'Duck Season Open' sign he finds. 'I am a duck bent on self preservation', he tells the audience, challenging the hunter/hunted order, as does Roald Dahl's 1968 story *The Magic Finger*, in which an eight-year-old girl discovers she can 'point a magic finger' at injustices and reverse reality. A friend's family shoots ducks: outraged, she points the finger at them – they shrink and grow wings. A family of ducks gains human arms, take over their house, sleep in their beds and threaten to shoot the humans with their own guns. In Michael Bedard's *Sitting Ducks* of 1998 (which began as a commercially successful poster before evolving into a picture book and an animated TV series), ducks roll off a factory assembly line worked by alligators. An egg drops off by accident, the emergent duckling secretly rescued by an alligator worker who at first plans to fatten it up for eating, but instead they become friends. The duck then cooks up a plan for the sitting ducks to flee Ducktown before they end up as meals. As with fairy tale, anthropomorphic humour 'points the finger' at human ironies, such as our tendency to imagine duck equally cheerily accepting its role as pet, friend or food. The duck's jolly personality disguises its

oppression. Works aimed at children in particular suggest the possibility of reading domestication as not slavery but a way to *rescue* duck from slaughter: a kind of agency-as-resignation. But how far were duck pressed into being domesticated?

THE PRESSED: DOMESTICATING DUCK

Neolithic cave drawings at Tajo de las Figuras in southern Spain show organized groups of hunted and possibly domesticated animals as part of a human settlement.

At La Cueva del Tajo de las Figuras in Andalusia, Spain, among over 500 Neolithic cave drawings at least 50 of the 178 birds are ducks. The cave is just 8 km (5 miles) from the shores of Laguna de la Janda, which has always been full of waterfowl. At the entrance to the cave are figures of women, children and men, including hunters and birds, filed like neat civil service records, of how many were caught: they are standing, walking and in flight. The drawings represent bird diversity as to size, species, type and behaviour. Are these roof and wall panels not only records of hunters and hunted but also of settlements, allotments, farmers: the first step in domestication?[18] Were some of these birds caught, owned, bred? Exchanged and traded? Could these drawings describe nomadic hunter-gatherers as they turn agriculturalists, marking out a borderline in the continuum of cultural adaptations, 8,000–15,000 years ago?

In the Las Figuras cave paintings there are line marks next to the rows of ducks. These juxtapose duck icons with numbers – suggesting three marks are three sets of something. Perhaps a scribe or notary marked down the weight and/or number of the commodity, on a document held by both parties to sanction and pledge the bargain? Thus depiction links directly to domestication. *The Walking Larder*'s definition of the 'essence' of domestication is the 'capture and taming of animals with particular behaviour characteristics, their removal from their natural living area and breeding community, and their maintenance

An Egyptian
poultry yard,
indicating the
early domestica-
tion of waterfowl,
in a fragment
of wall painting
from a tomb,
c. 1350 BC.

under controlled conditions for mutual benefits'.[19] Domestication can also be defined in anthropological terms: with ducks,
for example, being integrated into the socio-economic organization of human groups, as objects of ownership, inheritance,
exchange and trade.

Disagreement persists concerning Egyptian duck domestication, with the argument that there is no definitive evidence to
suggest that ducks were domesticated, though almost certainly
captured and held in captivity. The large quantities of ducks
that seasonally passed through Egypt as well as those that
stayed all year round could lead one to conclude that the number of wild ducks was so large that augmenting this through
domestication was unnecessary. Yet Diodorus Siculus, writing
his exhaustive history 60–30 BC, contradicts this:

What excites most our wonder and deserves the greatest praise, is the industry shown by the rearers of fowls, geese and duck, who, not contented with the course of natural procreation known in other countries, hatch an infinite number of birds by an artificial process. Dispensing with the incubation of the hens, they with their own hands bring the eggs to maturity; and the young thus produced are not inferior in any respect to those hatched by natural means.[20]

This technique continues to be used by modern Egyptians. By country village custom, eggs are collected from the peasants and handed over to the rearers, who place them on mats strewn with bran. Merchants sell the stock, fed for the table, in market towns.

Egyptian palaces, villas and even modest peasant dwellings contained poultry yards and aviaries. Old Kingdom reliefs depict some of the earliest attempts to tame and raise birds, with poultry cages, illustrated as large structures filled with cranes, ducks, geese and pigeons. Bird behaviour – fighting, pecking, strutting, preening – is often shown with humour. Since the birds in ancient Egyptian art and literature were all seed eaters or grazers, the original rationale for duck trapping may have been to stop them robbing crops. It is possible that pet ducks were even mummified, but the remains – as with those of most birds – failed to survive the 4,000 years wait for rediscovery. The Nile Valley and Delta were and remain excellent havens for birds, and migratory and non-migratory birds have long been important sources of food there. The Egyptians left many scrolls about correct ways to hunt and pen, which influenced medieval hunting.

In Europe, with the breakup of the Carolingian Empire (the fifth- to ninth-century Frankish kingdoms, now Germany and France), local lords monopolized forest reserves and small game in warrens, a practice most successful in England after the Norman Conquest and in Gascony from the twelfth century. Under these terms of ownership, the peasantry were engaged for penning, breeding and releasing harvested duck in season, but could not hunt the land themselves, poach being subject to severe punishment.

In Jan Steen's *The Poultry Yard* (overleaf), a wealthy heiress shows off her ownership of species and breeds both long domesticated (barabantes, Breda fowl and Old Bearded Dutch) and new fangled (crested duck). Most of the ducks are white.

The trait white, a negative property in the wild, is positively valued in captivity by humans. Since it is a recessive trait, it is easy to develop a pure breeding stock of 'always sleepy' white ducks.[21] The white duck has signed away its wildness for the tamer behaviour and weaker condition associated with un-coloured plumage. The foremost painter of hunting scenes and still-lifes of dead game in eighteenth-century France, Jean-Baptiste Oudry, combined naive naturalism with theatrical effects (as in the white-on-white composition illustrated over-leaf). Purchased unseen by Oudry's patron Carl Gustav Tessin even before it could be shown in the Paris Salon of 1753, *The White Duck* is a gorgeous example of exceptional technical skill. The other whites – candle, cloth, wooden table-altar, pomander bowl, wall – cleverly establish an argument in relative whiteness and stillness, suggesting religious refinement: duck as sacrificial object. Or perhaps mythological object: a fallen Icarus, legs and wings pointing up, neck curled in the bottom of a question mark; or erotic: a fallen sexual object, white and virginal, legs splayed to show its sex, the 'v' indent below the tail lit and painted with sensual attention to detail.

Yet the most carefully, beautifully placed item in the paint-ing is the piece of paper bearing the artist's signature and date. Attached like a tag to the duck's foot by a piece of string, it floats

magically above, as if the duck has only just fallen and the paper, slightly crumpled, casting a pale and blurred shadow, is still in mid-air. This duck is a fallen angel, at once gorgeously sexualized and de-sexualized, an object of impossible purity, its eyes and beak closed in beatific peace – sleeping, rather than dead. The duck and the paper have fallen together in such a way that it is as if they are still falling and always will. It is a painting

Mary Cassatt's 1890s print *Feeding the Ducks*.

engineered to show off Oudry's skills in reproducing different materials, objects and shades of white in confident, convincing perspective, cheating life and death, defeating the laws of gravity and time. Appropriately enough, since *The White Duck* is about art and illusion, it has disappeared. Worth £5 million, the painting was stolen in 1992 from Houghton Hall, home of its owner, the Marquess of Cholmondeley, who hired a former Head of Scotland Yard's Fine Art Detective Unit to track it down. Until a detective does so, one of the few places you can see this duck is in this book.

European and especially British landscape and flower painters over the next three centuries produced increasingly sentimental, twee images of ducks in their natural or domesticated

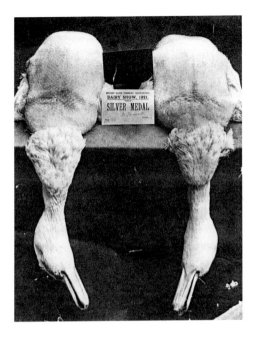

Aylesbury duck were declared the 'universal favourite' for eating by the cook Mrs Beeton in 1859. A pair of prize-winning ducklings exhibited in 1921.

habitat: *Duck and Ducklings by a Pond* by John Frederick Herring (*c.* 1795), George Frederick Nicholls's *Gloucestershire Village* (*c.* 1908), Thomas MacKay's *Feeding the Ducks* (*c.* 1913), Edgar Hunt's *Ducks by a Pond* (*c.* 1922). Latterly, these ducks were generally Aylesbury ducks or 'English Whites', a breed developed in the villages of Buckinghamshire around Aylesbury. According to Victorian local historian Robert Gibbs, 'In the early years of the present [nineteenth] century, almost every householder at the "Duck end" of the town followed the avocation of a ducker.'[22] The 'duck end' of town (the poorer end) encouraged disease: 'The Asiatic cholera commenced in those parts of the locality where the principal part of the sewerage of the town terminates, and open ditches existed, a large surface of stagnant water, and where ducks and other animals are kept in dwellings and on the premises of inhabitants.'[23]

Aylesbury ducks are large, with extremely white feathers, orange feet and pale pink beaks. They were bred to be eaten as eight- to ten-week-old ducklings, at weights of 2–3 kg (5–7 lb): hence the young were fed several times a day in their first week on eggs, toast, rice and liver, moving by the second week to a rich diet of barley meal, rice and tallow scrap ('greaves'), with some green vegetation, since without that it was observed the ducklings became giddy, fell over repeatedly and died. In their drinking water Aylesbury ducks were given grit from local flint, chalk pellets and pebbles, which gave the bills their characteristic fleshy colour. Killed on the premises, the ducklings were quickly hung upside down so the blood ran into the head, which kept the flesh white. It is not without irony, perhaps, that many of these scenes of ducks 'at home' or on ponds – so charmingly painted and photographed – may well have been the one swim the feasts-to-be ever had: 'It was a very pretty sight to see a flock of young ducklings driven along the village streets to have their one and only swim on a pond; which, taken at the right time, helped them to feather properly.'[24]

Beatrix Potter's Jemima Puddleduck is also an Aylesbury duck,[25] by 1908 a breed in some danger. At the height of the Aylesbury duck's reputation, in the 1850s, it was said to be the tastiest in the country, and thousands were sent to London for restaurants and quilt filling. In the first edition of *The Book of Household Management* (1859), the pioneer domestic goddess Mrs Beeton warmly recommended the killing and eating of Aylesbury ducks for the nation's gratification:

The white Aylesbury duck is, and deservedly, a universal favourite. Its snowy plumage and comfortable comportment make it a credit to the poultry yard, while its broad and deep breast, and its ample back, convey the assurance that your satisfaction will not cease at its death.[26]

In 1880 Aylesbury Dairy Company shares were known as 'ducks' on the London Stock Exchange, but, as a cheaper market-ready duck than the 'pure-breed' Aylesbury, the 'Peking' duck had been introduced into the UK and the US from China, and cross-bred with the Aylesbury. With rising duck food costs, problems arising from interbreeding, complacency and neglect (of ducks) came a decline in the Aylesbury industry, and by the Second World War most breeders had given up on it. As for duck eggs,

Beatrix Potter's Jemima Puddle-duck, blissfully ignorant of the dangers of the 'foxy gentleman'.

'The Brigade's Ducks', a popular 1960s Chinese poster, shows children at the edge of a lake watching a plenitude of white duck.

they went out of fashion in Europe after the war, along with the egg-laying breeds of duck. Hens' eggs became mass-produced and cheap, and several notorious cases of salmonella poisoning in the 1920s had implicated the duck egg. Duck meat, however, remained as popular as it is today.

Among others, Dutchman Constant Artz (1870–1952) answered the huge nineteenth-century demand for cute duck genre painting with works such as *Duck Family in a Meadow*, *The First Swim* and *Ducks in a Riverbank*. His birds bask in sunlight; light plays on their feathers, bathed in Impressionist splashes of yellow light, darling little ducklings bobbing in the water. The reality for the European domesticated duck was disease, force-feeding and one swim before slaughter.

From ancient Egypt and Rome to imperial China and Japan, in the Aztec empire, everyone everywhere ate duck. Ducks were domesticated for eggs, meat and feathers by the ancient Chinese and Maya and by early farmers in the Americas and Europe. Eating and sex are naturally analogous across many cultures' depictions of duck: Dutch genre paintings of kitchen scenes are often less a larder than an orgy of fish, fowl and meat. In these pictures, meat is a metaphor for all the pleasures of

Spilled fruit, the cat stalking the other dead duck, the hunter's gun against the wall – all contribute to Nicolaes Maes's allegorical *Woman Plucking a Duck*, 1655–6.

the flesh. If domestication accentuates the duck's capacity to be a symbol, then cookery accelerates this power towards a carnival chaos of symbolic capacity. Generally, if a pictured kitchen maid accepts a hunter's advances, duck will be on the menu. In Nicolaes Maes's *Woman Plucking a Duck*, a cat stalks the dead mallard, seemingly unnoticed by the servant woman, though dishes, bowl and basket are overturned, fruit pointedly spilled on the tiled floor. The hunter's weapon leans large and erect against the wall, suggestive of direct correlations between shooting and sexual arousal, hunting and sex.[27]

The eating of fertilized duck egg with a nearly developed embryo – *balut* – meaning 'wrapped' in Filipino, known in China as *maodan* (literally 'hairy egg'), has been common practice since the sixteenth century: Filipinos, Chinese, Cambodians and Laotians eat it as a street snack, or in the best restaurants. *Balut* is sold all the time and everywhere on streets, at stalls, outside movie houses, nightclubs or discos, in markets; by vendors walking, sitting or squatting, at midnight and early dawn, at breakfast, lunch and dinner time. The newly cooked *balut* are sold with twists of rock salt in baskets covered with cloth to keep them warm. *Balut* has an important role in Asian culture, where – perhaps because the egg is a fertility symbol – fertilized duck egg is thought to improve the male sex drive; in Filipino: *para lang sa lalaki ito* (it is just for men). Socio-cultural factors dominate its consumption. Men down two or three hot boiled eggs with cognac, drinking the egg white and quickly crunching the bones, feathers and beak of the foetus chick. Anthropologists suggest that 'machismo' arrived with the Spanish invasion of 1521 and that *balut*'s sexual connotation and promise of aphrodisiac properties derive from this, but local beliefs about its power also apply to women.[28]

A fifteen-day *Balut* egg boiled for a quarter of an hour shows the duck foetus floating in hot sauce and patis.

Consuming ducks' eggs and meat continues to relate to sexual health. The Jin-Ling black-beaked duck – a small, upstanding hybrid between the 'rare medical duck seeds of China and wild duck' – has been used to help relax the nerves, beautify the countenance and protect the liver, spleen and stomach since the Yuan Dynasty (1279–1368). Today, this duck, bred by the Nanjing Livestock and Poultry Research Institute for modern science and technology, of 'original and delicious taste' can

> prevent hepatitis, unknown fever, measles and so on . . . anchor your vim, keep your energy, nourish your marrow, accelerate your circulation of blood and make you stronger and cleverer than before . . . the refined product from the duck is useful for male impotence and the female menopause . . .[29]

Peking duck, introduced into the UK and USA from China, became the most popular duck among diners.

In ancient times duck meat was reserved for emperors. Peking duck is a famous duck dish from north-eastern China, still popular in Chinese restaurants around the world, and probably the best-known duck recipe, as the court dish of the Northern Song Dynasty (960–1127). First, the fresh plucked duck is inflated, separating the skin from the body (this was done by blowing through a straw by someone with strong lungs in ancient times). Boiling water is poured over the duck, hung up to dry overnight. Next day the skin may be brushed with honey before roasting in a hot oven for one or two hours. The bird is shredded, slivers of crisp skin and meat placed in the centre of a thin pancake with strips of cucumber, spring onions and a thick soy sauce, rolled up, and eaten with the fingers. A soup made with cabbage and the carcass may be drunk at the end of the meal. In 1873 a Yankee clipper reached Long Island carrying nine Peking (*Anas platyrynchos* or white mallard) ducks taken aboard in China. It is said that from these nine all the millions of Peking ducks in the US today are descended. The Peking is sturdy, tasty, juicy and – given that ducks generally have dark meat – has relatively light flesh.

The cultivation of the duck's own liver for *foie gras* (literally, 'fat liver') goes back to Egyptian antiquity, and the Romans force fed ducks with figs. The Roman emperor Heliogabalus allegedly fed his dogs on *foie gras* during the four years of his chaotic reign. References to *foie gras* appear in numerous Roman sources such as Cato, Martial, Pliny, Horace and Apicius, the last a fourth-century gourmet credited with compiling the only extant Roman cookbook. After the fall of the Roman empire, the tradition was preserved by the Jews, who carried the knowledge of *foie gras* with their migrations north and east to Europe. Penned birds were fed by scattering grain inside their enclosure, but there is also evidence that they were hand or force fed, to fatten or enlarge their livers, a practice familiar in France since medieval times, originating in the Perigord region. Probably farmed first by the Amerindians of the southern shores of the Caribbean and Peru, the muscovy duck has been cross-bred since the mid-nineteenth century across France, Israel, Taiwan, Australia and South Africa with other domestic ducks to producing sterile offspring – 'mules' or mulards – which mature quickly and taste excellent. In France

Forcible feeding of poultry in Egypt, from a tomb at Saqqara of C. 2,000 BC.

A can of *foie gras*, now part of the protected gastronomic inheritance of France.

and Israel muscovy cross-breeds are bred commercially for *foie gras* as well as for breast fillets weighing 400 g (13 oz) each.

Large white mallard ducks with black flecks bred around Rouen, the so-called 'Barbary' species, *canard mulard* or *canard clair*, are the authentic breed used to make the locally renowned *foie de canard*. After fourteen weeks free-range existence, by seventeen weeks ducklings at Le Ferme des Roumevies in St-Crépin-et-Carlucet are dead meat. Tourists can visit the farm's pens, laboratory and workshop, for cooking tips and the tasting of different products. Twice a day, morning and evening, the birds are fed boiled corn from a mechanical feeder in the traditional funnel-shape, with a human feeder massaging their throat, enabling them to eat at first 250 g (9 oz), eventually 1 kg (2 lb) a day. Kept in large purpose-built pens, the ducks drink thirstily after *gavage*. To say ducks are naturally greedy is hopelessly short of the truth. Johnsgard noted a single wild Falkland flightless steamer duck (*Tachyeres brachypterus*) with more than 450 mussel shells in its crop and stomach[30] – this was a record, but perhaps there is truth in the argument French farmers make: namely, that if ducks could find in a day all the grain they are force fed under *gavage*, they'd eat it anyway.

Once the ducks achieve optimum size – still judged by hand by feeling the underside – they are killed instantly by electrocution, hung upside down and plucked by machine. Down and feathers are collected for duvets, cushions and linings. The birds are sterilized rapidly and cooked or conserved in various ways,[31] then packed in sterile tins for immediate distribution. The process can, of course, be speeded up still further – industrial battery farming, castrated duck, hormones to increase growth, force-feeding with flour – though the French insist this produces *un monstre de natur*. Chef Paul Aussignac of Club Gascon in London feels intensive production does not create

good quality *foie gras* (or anything else) and artisanal, free-range husbandry renders the mechanical horrors of *gavage* unnecessary. Feelings run high in the farming communities of France about EU laws insisting mechanical gavage is more sanitary than hand-feeding. In October 2005, amid fears that animal rights activists would try to ban it completely, *foie gras* was declared a national treasure. '*Foie gras* belongs to the protected cultural and gastronomical heritage of France' states the French Rural Code. The ethics of the practice remain controversial: to date it has already been banned in some twenty countries, including Israel, despite the key role the Jewish diaspora played in the spread of force-feeding throughout Europe.[32] The EU Scientific Committee Report of 1998 concluded force-feeding was detrimental to the welfare of birds, but this has since been contested by American Veterinary Medical Association research, which found no evidence of stress and warned against unnecessary anthropomorphism. The reluctant compromise is that the force-feeding of animals for non-medical purposes has been prohibited by the EU since 1999, *except where it is in current practice.* Nowadays, around 20,000 tons of *foie gras* are produced worldwide. The French contribute 70 per cent of this and make up 85 per cent of its global consumption, with Hungary, Bulgaria, the US, Canada and China as smaller producers and consumers.

DUCK *PRESSÉ*

If 'one man's meat is another man's poison', this is certainly true of ducks. Ancient alchemists prized duck for its poisonous, medicinal and aphrodisiac properties. Pliny describes some 54 different poisons, including the following: 'The blood of a duck found in a certain district of Pontus, which was supposed to live on poisonous food, afterwards used in the preparation of the Mithridatum (antidote), because it fed on poisonous plants and suffered no harm.' Ironically, Mithridates tried to commit suicide by poison and it failed, perhaps due to this antidote, so he made a soldier stab him to death.[33]

In the Far East black pudding or blood tofu is traditionally made with duck's blood, and in Europe's East, 'Czarnina', or duck's blood soup, is an old Polish recipe used at Easter. Since the case of three brothers who contracted bird flu after sharing the Vietnamese delicacy of raw duck's meat and blood, the World Health Organization (WHO) advises against eating such meals; a recommendation that may also affect the future of *canard pressé* (squeezing the blood out of a duck carcass with a special press to make consommé).

Pressé is the most pressed a duck can become. For the European gourmand the most famous place to eat *canard pressé* is the Tour d'Argent in Paris, an exclusive restaurant that keeps a record of every duck. In 1582 this elegant inn on the Seine opened its doors to the aristocracy and soon became so popular that duels were fought to get a table. The duck are from Châlons in the Vendée: the inhabitants – *maraichins*, descendents of Spanish emigrants – captured and domesticated marshland birds, and from them bred the Chalandais duck, as they still do. In the 1800s the great *maitre d'hotel* Frédéric created the ritual of *canard au sang a l'orange*, and decreed that each duck cooked be registered, since when every order is served with a card stating your duck's number. Thus no. 328 went to the Prince of Wales, later Edward VII, in 1890, while Emperor Hirohito ate no. 53211 in 1921. If you choose duck there today with a friend rich enough to join you, the *commis* will write 'one duck for two' on the

The duck-press and numbered duck order from the Paris restaurant La Tour d'Argent, in a 1920s postcard.

blackboard and a *canardier* will weigh a duck arrived that morning from Châlons. Tour d'Argent describes the process on a webpage titled: 'His Majesty the Duck':

> On the eve, in spite of its youth, or rather because of its very youth (from 6–10 weeks), the poor bird was unfeelingly strangled, then plucked by its assassins. Here, it has already been roasted 20 or so minutes. The *canardier* dashes away to present it to the guest before the ritual sacrifice . . . In three strokes of a razor-sharp blade, a fat duck, roasted 'a la gouette de sang' skewered on the end of a fork, [is] skilfully sliced into two portions: on one side, the wings and legs, on the other, the body. Then . . . the magic potion, cognac and madeira, are poured into a consommé of what is left of the duck's carcass, to impregnate a finely chopped liver. A drop of lemon juice, and finally, the juice from the press. Beat well, keeping time to the formula: at least 25 minutes. This is the time it takes the aiguillettes to transform. With 'soufflés' potatoes, it is a supreme dish. Later, the legs are served, well broiled with salad. This duck, still proposed at the Tour d'Argent, has made its way around the world.[34]

This is the supreme irony: duck making its way 'around the world' not on the wing, but on the Internet, via a restaurant's reputation.

Since ancient times duck has been a valued food commodity across the globe. Perhaps humans still have idealized images of wild duck flying across the world, hunted fairly, trapped without cruelty but, just as ducks are taken in by decoys, so are we trapped in our cultural and social nets. The history of hunting cannot be separated from human–animal interactions, human-

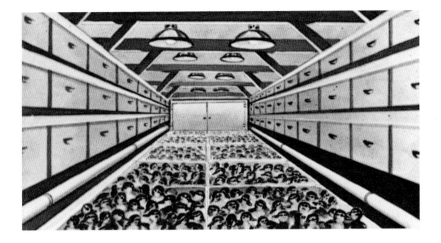

A futuristic vision of the 1970s that shows ducklings being reared in an incubator. This is now common practice, although the treatment of factory farmed duck has its critics.

ity and animality, nature and culture. Though hunting still requires some knowledge of 'free' nature, duck is easily domesticated to live among us 'as if' wild: in sanctuaries, parks, on farms, stately homes, even in our gardens as pets. Domesticated duck farmed to eat has been 'pressed' into a further compromised and contradictory relationship with us, via force-feeding to factory farming: that of a life caged 'inside' in the dark, hidden to the outdoor world until it becomes meat. 'Eat vegetables and fear no creditors, rather than eat duck and hide', goes a cautious Hebrew proverb. A duck's worth is still considerable. According to the World of Cherry Valley, the UK's largest duck farming company:

> duck can make a valuable contribution to alleviating the world's shortage of protein . . . helping to conserve the world's diminishing resources, for virtually everything from the feathers to the feet can be turned into profit. The liver, the tongue and even the feet all find a

ready market, while the world demand for feathers is increasing so rapidly that the net return from this by-product is alone sufficient to pay the labour costs of a processing plant. So nothing about a Cherry Valley duckling is unsaleable – not even the quack.[35]

3 The Duck's Quack

Wind and rain are on the way if ducks hiss and quack more than usual.
English superstition

By noting down their business transactions trappers and traders, converting wild ducks into commodities, oversaw the birth of the duck as symbol. Pai Ta-shun calls ducks 'runes' in his poem 'Wildfowl':

Dark flying rune against the western glow,
It tells of the sweep and loneliness of things,
Symbol of Autumns vanished long ago,
Symbol of coming Springs.[1]

In fact, the duck features repeatedly in sacred carvings, and not just as itself. Student scribes in Egypt drew practice hieroglyphs on stones called *ostraca* (cheaper than papyrus, which needed special preparation). Once trained and skilled, they continued to sketch or doodle cartoons for some of the more elaborate hieroglyphs.

Though linguists argue that the relationship between the signifier and the signified is 'arbitrary' (e.g. that the word 'tree' is not tree-like in sound), this does not appear to be true of duck. Duck seems to be a non-arbitrary name, based on duck sound and action. A *duck* in English is a word for a swimming bird, from the Old English *duce* mixed with *ducan*, meaning to dive or duck down. In Middle English the word became *douke*,

doke or *dukke* from the Norse, meaning doll or baby. Middle Low German is *duken*, Dutch *duiken*, Middle High German *tucken*, Old High German *tuhhan* and modern German *Tauchen* and *Ducken*. Words for 'duck' are musical and onomatopoeic in many languages: *mitiq* in Inupia (an Eskimo language), *ordek* in Turkish, *batakh* in Urdu, *pato-itik* in Cebuano (from the Philippines) and *bata-miti rangi-mbili* in Swahili. In hieroglyphic dictionaries we find, as well as definitions, suggested pronunciations of various duck hieroglyphs. As sound and icon slip past simile towards metaphor, the ducks vanish into the air.

There are schools of thought that maintain that language began with metaphor. 'Figurative language was the first to be born; proper meanings were the last to be found. If the first metaphor was animal, it was because the essential relationship between man and animal was metaphoric.'[2] In one of the most influential studies on animal language, the Gardners' work with chimpanzees,[3] a now famous experiment appears. To 'name' the first duck she saw to humans teaching her sign language, the chimp Washoe signed 'water + bird'. Of course, this does not tell us what 'duck' is in chimp, since she was doing it to communicate to the linguists she was working with, but it was

The duckling hieroglyph. The solar disc is a title of the king, the duck hieroglyph means both 'duck' and 'son'; therefore 'Son of Re'.

a 'novel combination', just as humans are capable of making. In fact, what follows is a near-exhaustive list of human novel combinations across the Anglophone world, in response to the word 'duck'. These fall into categories; the first of which, like Washoe, links duck to liquid pursuits:

The ancient game of 'ducks and drakes' or 'Menicus Felix: a kind of sport or play with an oister shell or a stone throwne into the water, and making circles yer it sink, &c. It is called a duck and a drake, and a halfe-penie cake', and is still played today by anyone throwing a flat stone obliquely to skim and rebound repeatedly from the water's surface:

> If the stone skims only once, it is a duck;
> twice: a duck and a drake, thrice, and a half-penny cake;
> four times: and a penny to pay the old baker;
> five times, a hop and a scotch, is another notch;
> six times, slitherum, slitherum, take her.

The 'ducking-stool', a test or punishment for witches. Note the ducks upstream observing human cruelty.

Sign for *The Dog and Duck*, a famous pub in London's Soho.

While a ducking-stool proved a woman was a witch (or that she was not, if she drowned), 'ducking' could also be drinking: to *drink with the ducks* is to drown in the sea: 'A goodly number would drink their grog with the Ducks tomorrow morning.' *Drunk as a duck* is very drunk: 'He's drunk as a duck and don't give a quack.'[4]

English inns and pubs have been named after ducks since *The Dog and Duck* signalled a hunter's stop in the fifteenth century. Guy Fawkes met the other gunpowder plotters at *The Duck and Drake* on The Strand in London; *The Dirty Duck*, a well-known actors' pub in Shakespeare's Stratford, provides the title of a crime novel by Martha Grimes that explores the bloodier side of Elizabethan verse. The disciplinary court of the British Stock Exchange from 1815 to 1870 was called the *Duckery*, while George Godfrey records the terms *to duck it*, *lame duck* and *waddle out as a lame duck* in his 1828 autobiography;[5] such expressions were probably then carried by colonists, emigrés or deportees to Australia, flowering into fresh local idiom. Sailors

The first successful seaplane was Henri Fabre's 'Le Canard'. Flown by its inventor at Martigues in France, the biplane's first flight in 1910 was 503 metres (1,650 feet).

or marines are still derisively referred to as *ducks* or *duckboys*: 'You'll find the ducks in the bar.' But there are other possible routes of derivation: Harrow School's swimming pool was known as the *duck paddle* or *ducker* until 1878; a *ducker* was also a sporting dive. Watery vocabulary is awash with duck terms, *duck diving* is a surfing term for pushing down on the beak and tail of a surfboard, going beneath a breaking wave. In Australian and New Zealand English – though of Irish origin – *duck weather* is very wet ('fine weather for ducks' is an ironic UK English phrase for the same). In France when freezing cold, *il fait un froid de canard*, and drenched to the skin is *trempe comme un canard*.

Frequently implying sexual derogation, duck idiom often satirizes gaming or play linked to masculine pursuits. Despite this, the overwhelming majority of metaphors stem from the collective noun or singular female 'duck', not the male 'drake'. The second category continues an already emerging masculine tone, drawing from military and sporting usage. A significant number of duck metaphors originate in military terms: in the First World War a two or a deuce in poker was a *duck*; *duck-shovelling* was to pass the buck; a *duck slop jar, glass duck* or *piss duck* was a hospital bedpan; a *duck butt* was a lighted cigarette stub; and *shooting ducks* was the action of relighting a previously extinguished cigarette butt: 'Duck that butt'. (*Duck buddies* shared their butt ends.) *Duck cloth* is the hardwearing cotton canvas that sea bags and boat covers were made of. *Duckboard* is military planking, as found in the trenches; a *duckboard harrier* was a messenger; a *duckboard glide* an after-dark movement along a trench. By the Second World War a *duck* was a sailor's uniform and an amphibious aircraft, or an aeroplane that was old and unreliable: 'This duck is about to fall apart!' *Seagoing ducks* were the enormous, cargo-carrying vehicles that unloaded ships, from the official acronym DUKW (the factory serial letters, combined, for boat, D, lorry body, U, and lorry chassis, KW). The Commando Armoured Car was nicknamed 'the Duck'. In army slang, to have *duck's disease* is to be short, a *duck shoot* is a simple operation, a *sitting duck* an easy target, a *dead duck* a craft dead in the water, a *duck pond* is a bathing place for cadets and a *column of ducks* is a line of soldiers.

Many of these alliterative, rhyming or onomatopoeic expressions may use the term 'duck' because of how satisfying it is phonetically: *ducks and drakes* is the shakes in Australian rhyming slang, *ducks and geese* the police, a *duck's neck* a cheque. A *blue duck* is a dud; *couldn't head a duck* is how you insult a racehorse. A *lame duck* cannot or will not pay his losses: 'He'll have to waddle out of the alley like a lame duck.' A *dying duck* or a *duck in a thunderstorm* is a crestfallen sight. To *duck the scone* is to plead guilty in court; *duck-shoving* is fighting for status; *shove that against your duck-house* is idiom for point scoring.[6] A duck can be a loser in any sport: 'I'm embarrassed to get in the ring with this unrated duck', Muhammad Ali said of Willi Besmanoff in a Louisville TV programme before their heavy-weight title fight in 1961. In radio and TV sports commentary, taking an idea from the fairground, to line one's ducks up is to be prepared, to have a strategy: 'He's lining up his ducks for his next move'; 'I bet he's got all his ducks in a row.' The terms *duck* or *goose egg* – indicating the zero shape – are obsolete in US English, but in the UK a *duck* can be a no-score in cricket, when you're out without making runs. If you're out very first ball, it's a *golden duck*, so some players wear ties proudly patterned with ducks.

The third category is sexual, on a continuum from affection-ate to obscene usage. In Geoffrey Chaucer's dream poem *The Parliament of Fowles*, a huge gathering of bird species debates, on Valentine's Day, attitudes to love. Conflicting authorities are addressed, in 'huge noyse', full of discord and complaint. The poem, written between 1373 and 1385, is thought to be an alle-gorical metaphor of the social discontents that gave rise to the Peasants' Revolt in 1381. But the duck has a comic role, inter-rupting matters with an apparently nonsense commentary irrel-evant to the argument: 'That men shulde loven alwey causeles!/ Who can a resoun fynde or wit in that?/ Daunseth he murye that is myrtheles?/ Who shulde recche of that is recheles?'[7] Moll Flanders goes into the streets of seventeenth-century London, not at night like any common prostitute, but in the beautifully ambiguous 'duck of an evening'.[8]

A century and a half later Dickens was a frequent duck metaphorist, though he uses it so lightly the reader can pass by without noticing. In *Barnaby Rudge* they are comic relief: 'Good night, noble captain', whispered the blind man – 'Good luck go with you for a conceited, bragging, empty-headed, duck-legged idiot.'[9] In *The Pickwick Papers* they are parodic reportage: during a court proceeding in which Sergeants Buzzfuzz and Snubbins interrogate witnesses in the incomprehensible vocabulary of the constabulary, Susannah Sanders is forced under oath to admit:

> During the period of her keeping company with Mr Sanders, [she] had received love letters, like other ladies. In the course of their correspondence Mr Sanders had often called her a 'duck', but never 'chops', nor yet 'tomato sauce'. He was particularly fond of ducks. Perhaps if he had been as fond of chops and tomato sauce, he might have called her that, as a term of affection.[10]

Dickens exposes how terms of endearment can turn sinister, as in *The Old Curiosity Shop*, where the dwarf Quilp refers to the lovely child Nell as 'dainty duck' and 'my duck of diamonds', a duck ornament he covets and keeps while she weeps for her dying father.[11] In modern UK English a duck can be a fine example of something: 'Oh, isn't he the duck of a fellow?' A *duck of diamonds* is the best, as is the *duck's quack*. *Duck Soup* – besides being the title of well-known comedies by Laurel and Hardy in 1927 and the Marx Brothers in 1933 – is anything easy, a guaranteed success. 'I went a-ducking with my duck' is to go courting with a sweetheart. Though Henry VIII's letter to Anne Boleyn uses *duckys* to mean her breasts – 'whose pritty duckys I trust shortly to kysse'[12] – *ducky*, slang from 1897, expressed general fondness, especially as still used in the East Midlands of England: 'Isn't that ducky?' 'How are you, duckie?' 'Alright, me duck?' By the early twentieth century, in Australian English, it had become male and sarcastic – 'Isn't that a ducky pair of shorts?' – and a similar usage is found in present-day gay communities, often for exaggerated, camp irony. This may carry crudely homophobic overtones: 'Watch your ass: there's duck dudes round here', and *duck* became US slang for 'gay'.[13] In Mandarin Chinese a duck or *yazi* is a male prostitute. Yet, as noted in the categories above, many duck metaphors are associated with the seemingly manlier pursuits of competitive sports and military action. What begins to be apparent is how untrustworthy duck idiom is, how it itself ducks fixed categories of meaning.

US slang has a *duckbutt* as a runt; a *duck's ass* (or *DA*) a 1950s haircut; *a duck-fucker* a loafer or lout (named after the man who looked after the poultry on a warship); a *duck fit* is a tantrum; a *duck fart* the plop of a stone falling into water; the exclamation 'Fuck a duck!'[14] expresses astonishment; the *duckpond* is the vagina; *duck butter* is smegma, semen or sweat around the male genitals; to *stick the duck in the mud* is a (male) plan to have sex.

Some duck metaphors remain elusive. If *duck green* is the bright green of duckweed, *duck-egg blue,* the palest, purest light greenish-blue thought by some to be the colour of infinity, perhaps refers back to those myths of a world created from a cosmic duck's egg. In Caribbean Hinglish *duck-pickneys* are ducklings: the expression 'Hen 'gree fe hatch duck egg, but him no

In South Africa to 'duck in the green curtains' is to sleep on the slopes of Table Mountain.

'gree fe teck duck-pickney fe swim' ('Hen may have agreed to hatch duck's egg, but did not agree to take the ducklings swimming') ironically queries family expectations and arrangements.[15] So wide-ranging are these many meanings, commonsense guesses at lost colloquialisms are simply impossible. In the colloquial Anglo-Indian of 1787 one purwannah of Tipoo Sultan declared: 'We have fixed the produce of each vine at four ducks of wet pepper.'[16] What on earth *these* ducks might have been – sacks? buckets? ducats? – is lost to us.

In Farrukh Dhondy's 1990 novel *Bombay Duck*, a black Jamaican is taken by an Indian friend to London's Brick Lane Market, famous for its curry houses:

> He comes back with this thing which looked like the penis of an opened-up mummy I saw in a museum once. 'Your Bombay duck,' and he pops it on the table. 'I said duck, man, not shrivelled insoles.' The thing was stinking. Anjali was looking amused . . . 'We Indians call that duck. Bombay duck.' Smell like salt fish gone bad. 'That's what it is. Try it.' Bwoy, I was too polite to say what it taste like. A fish called duck, cool, well, you live and learn, boss.

Bombay duck is 'a fish called duck': a small marine lizard fish native to Bombay abundant in the Ganges delta and Arabian Sea, dried and salted whole or filleted, used as a relish, especially with curry. Locally (in Hindi) the fish is known as 'bombil',

Bombay duck, actually a deep sea lizard fish (*Bathysaurus ferox*).

'bomnaloe macchi' or 'bummalo': there are various stories how it came to be 'Bombay duck', either, during the Raj, the Victorian British were embarrassed at the rude-sounding 'bummalo' or:

> when the British introduced the railway system to western India under their Raj, it started going in wagonloads to the interior from Bombay. The crates stank of fish, like stale penises. They were marked 'Bambay Dak', literally 'Bombay Mail'. At the time the railway was run by whiteys. The English may call a spade a spade but they don't call 'stinking fish' by that name. They referred to it euphemistically as Bombay Dak.[17]

Dhondy uses Bombay duck as an extended metaphor to expose British hypocrisy or sexual, cultural and linguistic double standards; 'spade' being a racist term for Blacks of African origin. As further irony, Bombay duck was banned for a while by the European Commission, because it is dried in the open air – since reprieved for export to the UK if sealed in approved packing stations.

The final category has 'ducking' as a special kind of moving, a furtive, ironic 'slip' between one thing and another (arguably, just as metaphor works). As Milton put it: 'Here be, without duck or nod / Other trippings to be trod.'[18] It can mean a slight bow: 'The learned pate ducks to the golden fool', said Shakespeare.[19] In plain verb usage, 'to duck' means a sudden inclination of the head or body, resembling the motion of a duck in water. To *duck* something is to avoid it: 'We made an excuse for duckin' church'; in the army to *duck a detail* is to shirk work; Cockney *duck and dive* rhymes with 'skive'; to *duck someone* is to avoid them surreptitiously: 'We meets Charlie ducking

Cross-Euro duck metaphors: the (French) Citroën 2CV car is (to the Dutch) *een eend* (a duck).

into a beanery', 'Come on, quick, let's duck!' In espionage a *duck dive* is a period of bad mistakes; to *duck out* is to escape capture. A dark corner is a *duck* to hustlers – an easy place to rob; to *do a duck* or *play the duck* or *fake the duck* is to leave without or avoid paying a fare; to *cop a duck* is to lay low, out of sight. The duck's own movement – waddling – is part of this comic word-play: the Vietnamese have idioms for being 'duck-legged', *baata* is duck in Bantu (a group of languages of Central and Southern Africa) and *baatabaat* to waddle like a duck; in Italian *caminare come un anatra*. In German *Blaue, felte Ente* is false or unfounded information used in journalism; in French, *un canard* can be a lump of sugar soaked in coffee or alcohol, a slip or mistake, inaccurate information or a hoax: *Le Canard enchaine* is a satirical newspaper, *lancer des canards* is to tell trumped-up stories, *vendre un canard a moitié* is to 'half-sell a duck', in other words, to cheat.

In parallel to the extraordinary diversity of human idioms about duck, the voices of actual duck vary enormously, hence the challenge in describing them. Modern scientists use the language of comic-strip onomatopoeia to describe the male musk duck's extraordinary courtship display: 'He also produces a variety of sounds during these PADDLE-KICK, PLONK-KICK, and WHISTLE-KICK displays, including KER-PLONKS . . . Both sexes of whistling ducks utter a clear, multisyllabic whistle . . . including a whirring sound produced by the wings in flight.'[20]

Published almost a century earlier, John C. Phillips's *A Natural History of the Ducks* is an impressive collection of amateur naturalist observations, revealing the tendency for humans to anthropomorphize onomatopoeically duck voice descriptions, from the 'South-south-southerly' song of the old squaw to the scoter who 'whistle with their wings' and make 'the sound of water dropping into a cavern: "puk-puk"'. Golden-eye are also called merry-wing, rattle-wing or jingler in English, *Klangente, Klingelente, Klapperente* in German or *morillon sonneur* in French because of the loud humming or whistling sound the narrowed web the last two primaries (ten outer quills in each wing) make as the drakes fly. Fulvous duck apparently make un-duck-like reedy whistles or flocking calls, described by Gibson in 1920 as 'the crackling of rain upon a hot iron-plate',[21] modifying their voices almost like singing birds and responding to imitations of their call-notes. *Dendrocygna bicolor* (the fulvous whistling duck) is called *pata quiriri* in Spain, *vis-sisi* in Guiana, *güiriri* in Venezuela and *tsiriry* in its native home, Madagascar; it is said to call 'pyswy-pyswy'. The notes of the teal are variously translated as: 'ek-ek', 'kup-kup', ruck-ruck', 'wot-wot-wot', 'mok-mok', even 'tick-tick' or 'clock-clock', or a creaking call like the 'low soft whine of a little puppy'. For the male steamer duck the range is from 'rasping grunts' via 'mechanical ticking' to 'whistle-like sibilant grunts'. In 1909 R. Hall described the same species of duck (freckled) with a voice like 'the grunt of a Berkshire pig' *and* 'the mewing of a cat'.[22] Harlequin ducks

A Peking duck's beak wide open, showing tooth-like ridges and tongue.

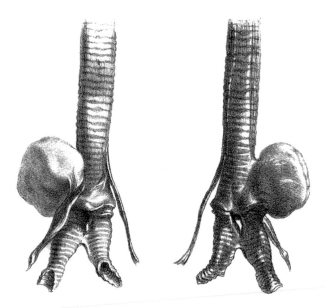

Thomas Eyton's drawings of duck trachea, showing the ossified enlargements at the union between the trachea and the bronchi, or 'bulla', which acts as a resonating body for sound production.

squeak like mice. Eider hoot like owls. The gentle voice of pochard, a 'soft, liquid, several syllabled utterance in chorus', is a call also described as 'somewhat like a man affected with asthma told by the doctor to take a deep breath'.[23]

The lists of duck sounds are clearly endless, but how does the creature manage this diversity of repertoire? Watch closely and you'll see the whole diaphragm move with a duck's voice, like an opera singer. That is why the duck can laugh (open beak laughs). Though the quack sound is overwhelmingly what ornithologists concentrate on, duck noise is actually made by the whole of a duck's body: it clicks, tuts, whispers, grinds, hisses, quacks and squawks with the beak from shut to wide open; caresses, curls, twists and taps with the head and neck; rustles, whirrs, hums and beats with the feathers on closed, outstretched

Cornix cornicatur,   *à à* A a
The Crow crieth.

Agnus balat,   *b è è è* B b
The Lamb bleateth.

Cicàda stridet,   *cì cì* C c
The Grashopper chirpeth.

Upupa dicit,   *du du* D d
The Whooppoo saith.

Infans ejulat,   *è è è* E e
The Infant crieth.

Ventus flat,   *fi fi* F f
The Wind bloweth.

Anser gingrit,   *ga ga* G g
The Goose gagleth.

Os halat,   *ha'h, ha'h* H h
The Mouth breatheth out.

Mus mintrit,   *ì ì ì* I i
The Mouse chirpeth.

Anas tetrinnit,   *kha, kha* K k
The Duck quacketh.

Lupus, ululat,   *lu ulu* L l
The Wolf howleth.

Ursus murmurat, *mummum* M m
The Bear grumbleth.

or flying wings; fans and shakes the tail feathers; flaps and slaps with webbed, waddling feet. Duck's elemental association with water repeats in idiom across many languages: taking to it as well 'as a duck to water'; things roll off 'like water off a duck's back'. Many of the noisier duck sounds are made with water: dabbling, splashing, washing, shaking, swimming, up-ending, diving, popping back up, defecating with a loud liquid squelch. One might say the duck has verbal diarrhoea.

Konrad Lorenz listed a number of categories of voice in 1953 based on mallard: 'inciting' (*queg-geg-geg-geg*), the 'decrescendo' or 'hail call' to attract (*quack-quack*), the whole performance of display, *rabrab palavar*, post-copulatory 'whistle', persistent quacking before laying, harsh *queggeggegegqueggegeg* or 'scolding' *gaeck* sounds to repulse unwanted male harassment, *tocka-ta-tockata* feeding sounds, auditory imprinting with *gn-gn'gn* and *quai-quai*, and *peep* cries from the young. Ducklings utter longer distress cries when wet, hungry, cold, alarmed or separated. Lorenz called this a 'whistle of desertion' and believed the male *raehb* note developed ontogenetically from this call. Less recorded than the louder duck sounds made in flight, display, mating or behaviour when excited or disturbed are the quiet, intimate sounds intended for the close group. The duck has an exquisite repertoire of subtle sounds – it even talks in its sleep.

'With a quack-quack here, a quack-quack there,/ Here a quack, there a quack,/Everywhere a quack-quack,/Old MacDonald had a farm. ee-i, ee-i, o!'[24] Things are patently not this simple: 'quacking' can be many things, most often scornful, linked, perhaps, to how a duck's quacking often sounds like derisory laughter to humans. Leonard Woolf's indictment of fascism and militant nationalism, *Quack! Quack!*, was described by Virginia Woolf as 'a very spirited attack upon human nature'. Published by the couple at the Hogarth Press in 1935, the book uses 'quacking' as equivalent to anti-Semitic ranting. Woolf demonstrates what he thinks of speeches and pamphlets by Hitler and Mussolini by ending quotes with two derisory words: 'Quack, quack!'[25] Muriel Sparks's 1960 *Ballad of Peckham Rye* has a wife dare to say 'That's how *you* go quacking on' to her self-important husband, with fatal results.[26] Though George Orwell's *1984* labels *Duckspeak* as quacking like a duck without thinking (as it is used in computer science), *duck typing* has recently developed as a term for the dynamic systems of some programming languages.

As is already evident, onomatopoeia is fundamental to duck's language history. Yet the sounds that humans *attribute* to duck are not rigorously scientific. The French – in different contexts – hear *coin-coin, couin-coiun, couan-couan, couean-couean* or even *can-can*. Typically, a rhythmic pair of strongly onomatopoeic words emerges: *cac-cac* (Vietnamese), *kac-kac* (Czech), *quack-quack* (English), *qua-qua* (Italian), *couak-couak* (Arabic), *kwek-kwek* (Dutch), *kvakk-kvakk* (Norwegian), *kva-kva* (Slovakian), *kwa-kwa* (Hebrew), *krya-kyra* (Russian), *kwrk-kwrk* (Mongolian), *kkoyk-kkoyk* (Korean), *gaab-gaab* (Thai), *ga-ga* (Slovenian), *gaa-gaa* (Japanese), *gua-gua* (Chinese), *gack-gack* (Bengali), *graz-graz* (Spanish), *gik-gak* (Esperanto), *rap-rap* (Danish), *hap-hap* (Hungarian), *hat-hat* (Iroquie), *mak-mak* (Albanian), *vak-vak* (Turkish), *sisip* (Cree).

For centuries, composers from Mozart to Stravinsky and Satie have been inspired by birdsong: for Olivier Messiaen, its transcription and mimicry was a central project. For works such as the *Catalogue d'oiseaux*, completed in 1958, and *La Fauvette des jardins* of 1971, Messiaen was considered a more conscientious ornithologist than any previous composer, and a more musical observer of birdsong than any previous ornithologist.[27] More recently, 'natural sound' music uses digital recordings

A screen-grab from *The Quack-Project*, a work by the author, which plays with onomatopoeic words that humans give to animal sounds.

of birds in their natural habitat to form 'audio collages'.[28] Contemporary composer John Levack Drever's *Quack Composition for The Quack-Project* features ducks quacking and children imitating them, then cut, pasted and mixed as looped rhythmic parts that still sound individual and unique: 'The extra-musical interest was the dialogue between human and animal, and the sounds that fall somewhere in-between.'[29] Players of the *The Quack-Project* can click on the duck icon to place them in the field where they will make a sound according to the chosen language, thereby creating compositions from duck sounds as they manifest in different languages spoken across London; a visual and aural reminder and celebration of the verbal, tonal and melodic diversity of kingdoms human and animal. Duck have different dialects too.

But the finest – and most utopian – example of musical duck metaphor in composed music is Messiaen's pupil Karlheinz Stockhausen's avant-garde electro-acoustic *Hymnen* (*Anthems*), its object – like the *The Quack-Project* – being nothing less than world harmony.[30] Listening to radio broadcasts from all over the world,

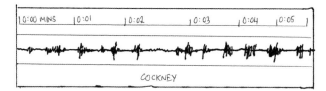

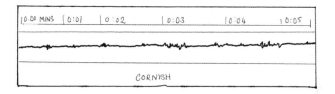

'Duck's Dialect(ic)': Sound files show clear differences between Cockney and Cornish ducks recorded in 2004.

Karlheinz Stockhausen's drawing of 'spatial polyphony' in his electronic piece *Hymnen* (1966–7) sees notes like ducks in a pond. (At one point in *Hymnen* sounds are manipulated so that a duck quacks the beginning of the *Marseillaise*!)

Stockhausen recorded over 150 national anthems, including *La Marseillaise*, being quacked rather than sung. He took the sounds of children playing, and put them through an electro-acoustic distortion process, turning them into swamp ducks:

little boys shouting 'Hi, come here!' – speeded up, and I moved this sound up again in speed until it sounds like ducks. I used an actual recording of swamp ducks, and you don't notice when the real ducks are continuing from the human voices. I then took one small duck – just a Quack-Quack – and put her on the machine, and she quacks the beginning of the *Marseillaise*: Quack-quak-quak-qua-qua, qua-qua, cah cah cah qua quaaa . . . I'm interested in revealing how, at a special moment, a human sound is that of a duck and a duck's sound is the silver sound of shaking metal fragments. Many of the fairy tales are about this: the straw that the miller's daughter has to weave into gold in *Rumpelstiltskin*, for example . . . And that's the theme of *Hymnen*.[31]

Just as Stockhausen's *Hymnen* plays with the language rules of national and universal music, linguists who have made studies of sounds in different languages argue that there are recognizable, rule-governed 'grammars of onomatopoeia'. The metaphors of duck as affectionate (love a duck), sexual (fuck a duck), criminal (duckin' and divin'), punningly playful ('duck or grouse' signs on low beams warning tall English country pub drinkers), or onomatopoeic ('drunk as a duck and don't give a quack') suggest that human wordiness around duck parallels the animal's own verbosity, slipping between scientific truth and expediency like quack-doctors.

4 Ducks *ex machina*: The Mechanical and Animated Duck

In the Musée des Rêves Mécaniques (Museum of Mechanical Dreams) in Grenoble, France, is a copy of a mechanical duck built by Jacques de Vaucanson, born in that city in 1709. Dubbed a 'new Prometheus' by Voltaire and La Mettrie, Vaucanson began his career developing new technologies for silk manufacture, but following a riot by angry silk workers (and pioneer Luddites), he fled to Paris, where he turned his attentions to automata. He exhibited the duck in 1739; it became his most famous creation: looking up 'automaton' in the early editions of Diderot's *Encyclopédie*, you would have found a description of Vaucanson's robot duck.

The same size as a *canard sauvage* (wild mallard), it was made of gold-plated copper, and could drink, dabble in the water with its beak, quack and flap its beautifully articulated wings. Each wing had over 400 articulated parts, meticulously copied from the duck in nature. It took food from Vaucanson's hand, swallowed it, digested it and – in front of amazed audiences – excreted it. It was the Age of Reason, and the inventor also provided detailed anatomical diagrams in lectures. Civilization cannot be separated from its waste: the duck was beyond a machine; it was a highly skilled joke.

Vaucanson died in 1782, his duck long flown. It had toured Europe with him, only to be pawned in 1754, bought by a

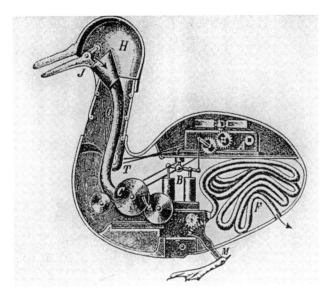

Vaucanson's duck, drawn in an attempt to grasp how it might digest its food. It was found out later not to work like this, but to 'trick' the viewer by eating and then defecating from separate mechanical parts.

German professor of philosophy and medicine who showed its wreckage to Goethe and refused an offer from Napoleon to buy it, found again years later in another pawnbroker's attic and eventually passed on to the famous Swiss clockmaker J. B. Reichsteiner, who made himself ill painstakingly repairing it over three and a half years.[1] A duck in working order was once more exhibited in 1843, but it is unclear whether this was the original or a copy – Reichsteiner had made another version, dressed with real feathers. Hence a copy of a copy (of a copy?): the duck on display today in Grenoble, made by the gifted automatist Frédéric Vidoni: a replica of a copy of a model of a real duck.

In order to distinguish animals from humans in terms of capacities and behaviours, the model of the machine is frequently used. The difference between the literal and the

116

metaphorical is based only on convention; what we take at one time or another to be (as if) alive or intelligent. In Vaucanson's time, the automated machine was as popular a metaphor to reflect on human life as the computer is today. Though writers such as Julien Offray de La Mettrie controversially argued that man was a 'self-winding machine',[2] the soul 'nothing more than an empty word to which no idea corresponds', the fact that *anima* means 'soul' suggests that the automata of Vaucanson's day were a means to humanize the machine.

Thomas Pynchon's epic novel *Mason & Dixon*, about the rich possibilities and tragedies in the founding of America as a nation, features the memorable character of Vaucanson's duck. Apparently, at the time Vaucanson was building the robot, he was suffering from a fistula of the anus, and could not eat – hence his obsession, perhaps, with robot bowels, anus and sphincter: 'Without the shitting duck', Voltaire commented, 'there would be nothing to remind us of the glory of France.'[3] In Pynchon's novel the Englishman Dixon recalls him as 'the Lad with the mechanickal Duck', but a French chef prefers rhetoric: 'the man Voltaire called a Prometheus, – to be remember'd only for having trespass'd so ingeniously outside the borders of Taste, as to have provided his Automaton a Digestionary Process, whose end result could not be distinguish'd from that found in Nature.' 'Soon Tales of Duck Exploits are ev'rywhere the Line may pass. The Duck routs a great army of Indians. The Duck levels a Mountain west of here. In a single afternoon, the Duck, with her Beak, has plow'd ev'ry field in the County, at the same time harrowing with her tail. That Duck!'[4]

Pynchon's picaresque fusing of real history and science with fable and folklore brings Vaucanson's duck literally to life where its (*real*) existence was a metaphor before. Literature animates what might have happened; science vivifies the mechanical; and the natural turns supernatural. Questions of animate reality that Vaucanson (by constructing and exhibiting the mechanical duck) was raising in an Age of Reason are toyed with, as the duck brings her 'erotick Machinery' to life. Questions of sexual power relations are recognized by the chef, who understands the politics of flesh: 'her Iron Confidence in the power conferr'd her by her Inedibility, being artificial and deathless, as I was meat'. *Not* believing in Vaucanson's duck has real risks. Mason criticizes his Age's (the nineteenth century's) need for artificial life, 'its Faith in a Mechanickal Ingenuity', but, as he refers to the duck as a 'French toy', his hat is swept high into the sky by an invisible creature, 'faint Quacking heard above'. 'Very well', Mason calls. '"Toy" may've been insensitive. I apologize. "Device"?'[5]

Vaucanson's 'device' was exactly what the word means: at once a cunning machine, a tool for change and a way of achieving something somewhat dishonestly. No wonder Pynchon used the duck as an ideal plot device to raise questions about historical reliability in the context of contemporary (artificial) life. The figure of the duck works dually: with consistent 'iron confidence' since it is animated artificially, and unstable 'soul' expressed in personality, exactly as was developed for the Disney device called Donald Duck.

With a workforce urgently directed to develop a brand new cultural technology, Walt Disney – the great satirist of the machine age – was nevertheless deeply suspicious of technology, as early animations demonstrate. A pastiche of Charlie Chaplin's 1936 *Modern Times*, *Modern Inventions* in 1937 had Donald Duck visit a 'Museum of Modern Marvels', get tied up by a wrapping machine, force fed and changed by an automated baby basket, turned upside down by an automatic barber chair that trims his tail feathers and shoeshines his face and beak, while a robot butler repeatedly reappears to swipe his hat. Of course, non-fictional ducks suffer exactly these indignities – they're trussed, dressed, force fed, clipped and controlled – but the fearful spectre of a dehumanizing technological modernity dissolves into familiar human–duck gags (such as the 'duck's arse' haircut). The threat of humanity-as-machine is dispelled by comic effect, since the machines become human and the put-upon human is a duck. Underlying this is a darker joke: the machines – as they are humanized – treat this duck/human as if he were a non-human (or 'real') duck.

Accused of much – the venom perhaps a measure of his titanic cultural stature – Disney is best seen as an instinctive populist, the 'triumph of the little guy' his deepest political ideal. In the early 1930s Disney was best recognized by a cartoon mouse, but:

> As the Depression began to wane, Mickey was surpassed in popularity by another character, the irascible Donald Duck. This was not completely an accident. Perhaps appealing to a recovered sense of social confidence in America by the late 1930s, the quick-tempered Donald captured audience's affection with an assertive, even belligerent determination to secure his place in the scheme of things. Displaying temper tantrums that were truly works of art and a squawking, half-intelligible voice that could raise the dead, the Duck burst into Disney's short films as a cocksure populist hero.[6]

Far more than Mickey, it is Donald – labelled 'a bad, a wicked duck, a malicious and mischievous duck, a duck corresponding to all the maddening attractiveness of bad little boys and girls' – that most expresses the shifting cultural climate in and beyond animation. Donald's voice was provided by a former circus clown, Clarence 'Ducky' Nash, whose vocal impressions were key to making the duck the success he was from 1934. Using nasal sounds and the full range of the mouth, the sound was a comic blend of quacking or squawking like a duck and a human child's manic excitement. The worse he behaved, the better the duck was liked. The Disney story department supervisor at this time was one George Drake, who was prey to rages: was Donald created by the design team to annoy him, or even modelled on him?

> After enduring a particularly obnoxious temper tantrum, they grabbed [Drake] from each side and lifted him off the floor, firmly goosed him while he screamed . . . carried him out of the building, and dumped him in the middle of Hyperion Avenue. They were sternly reprimanded of course, but that scarcely mattered in the light of the standing ovation they got from staff members who witnessed the incident.[7]

The propensity in cartoon to gratuitous violence worked in more than one direction – the very fact that anger was justified as funny made the humour politically effective. In 1941, when the Disney animators went on strike, they distributed a flyer aimed at the public: Donald pounds the floor in fury, screaming: "'This makes me mad! I've been making you folks laugh for years and years, but now something has happened that ISN'T FUNNY AT ALL . . .". The flyer put the worker's case, from Donald Duck's point of view.'[8] Walt himself was convinced that the strike was led by communists – and said as much to the FBI and others. The workers won the strike that same year, but Walt had his revenge on the treacherous duck. As war concerns mounted,

US military personnel moved in, and the studio was commissioned to make a series of educational war films on behalf of the Government. On 1 March 1942 Walt gave a radio speech entitled 'Our American Culture', broadcast during the intermission of a performance at the New York Metropolitan Opera: 'It is the constitutional privilege of every American to become cultured or just grow up like Donald Duck. I believe that this spiritual and intellectual freedom which we Americans enjoy is our greatest cultural blessing.'[9]

'Donald Duck Work for Victory' said a headline: the Disney war effort began with *Donald Gets Drafted* in 1942, and the duck marched on through *Commando Duck*, *The Old Army Game*, *Sky Trooper* and *Home Defense*. To encourage the payment of income tax during wartime, the US Government invested in a Disney cartoon bearing the slogan 'Taxes to Beat the Axis'. Donald had little American flags for eyes, and it was a success with critics, public and the Treasury Department alike. It is easy to imagine the current US Government wishing Disney could be brought back to life . . .

The most successful of Disney's wartime films, winning an Academy Award, was *Der Fuehrer's Face* of 1943. Donald dreams he works in a munitions factory in totalitarian 'Nutziland'. As the dream becomes a nightmare of food shortages and the ever-faster fixing of bomb parts, he screams 'I can't stand it, I'm going nuts!' – and explodes. In a surreal sequence, *he* becomes the object moving down the assembly line, shell casings battering him, until at last he sees the Statue of Liberty. 'Am I glad to be a citizen of the United States!' he squawks in relief.

After the war, when family values took precedence over military ones, the 'Disney Doctrine', as it has since been called, made its films not simply as suitable for family viewing, but also explicitly 'true to the American family', and this

Poster for *Der Fuehrer's Face*. One in the eye for Hitler from the Disney team in 1943.

met with great commercial success. Before 1954 Donald was never part of a recognizable family unit, but a 'domesticated, middle-class, fatherly fowl' appeared in *Spare The Rod*, where Uncle Donald gets a lesson in child psychology with nephews

Huey, Louie and Dewey, and *Donald's Diary*, where a now-sub-urban Donald considers marriage to Daisy Duck. Not used by Disney for animations after the late 1950s, the Donald Duck character was to be the star of the *Donald Duck* magazine for years to come.

Jack Bradbury, Phil de Lara, Jack Moores, Paul Murry, Tony Strobl and Al Taliferro all drew the duck – alongside countless unnamed inkers and colourists – but the most famous writer and artist pair was Bob Karp and Carl Barks. A rare Barks litho-graph would now fetch around $15,000. Donald remains as popular as he is collectable.

In Roy Lichtenstein's *Reflections: Portrait of a Duck*, 1989, Donald sees and speaks nothing but money.

'If it looks like a duck, walks like a duck, and quacks like a duck – it's a duck,' said McCarthyists, talking about communists. According to Ariel Dorfman's and Armand Mattelart's famous rage against the Disney machine,[10] Chile's class enemy was Donald Duck: 'As long as Donald Duck strolls with his smiling countenance so *innocently* about the streets of our country, as long as Donald is power and our collective representative, the bourgeoisie and imperialism can sleep in peace.'[11] *How to Read Donald Duck* insisted: 'Disney uses animals to trap children, not to liberate them.'

Donald has become emblematic of the question: how far is life a 'product'? The duck as consumer object par excellence; commodified, commercialized, world-famous. Pop artist Roy Lichtenstein said of the Disney Ducks: 'I really love their stupidity.'[12] Every animated or cartoon duck reference is deliberately superficial and derivative, like George Orwell's greedy proles in *1984*: unthinking ducks, robot rabble useful only as automata like Vaucanson's: 'They simply swallowed everything, and what they swallowed did them no harm, because it left no residue behind, just as a grain of corn will pass undigested through the body of a bird.'[13]

Blurring the boundaries between human and duck is increasingly popular. One of the most successful 'anime' series to date, Rumiko Takahashi's comedy manga *Ranma nibun no ichi* (*Ranma ½*) has a central character who transforms into a girl when doused with water. The same charmed water turns his rival friend, Mousse, into a fighting duck. *Ranma ½* originated in 1987 as an animation aimed at Japanese children or youth culture, particularly boys, but its interest and collectability is now global in scale.

Still instantly recognizable, Donald Duck continues to be a touchstone for present-day artists, forming an exhibition in

2004 at the Cobra Museum of Contemporary Art in The Netherlands, to mark 70 years of his existence. German artist Gottfried Helnwein interviewed Carl Barks in 1992 when – after 50 years of it – Barks said he wouldn't paint another duck. Asked about his 'beautiful human girls with real breasts' for 1980s *Xerxes and Harem*, Barks admitted: 'Yes, that one got me into trouble . . . I had to spend several hours in the art editor's office in order to flatten all the breasts . . . and the girls had to have dog or duck faces.' By contrast, Helnwein, free from corporate censorship, paints canvases of the duck with film noir gangsters and naked ladies, or on the street, in blue-tinted black

In *American Prayer*, 2000, Gottfried Helnwein sees Donald Duck as 'a small artificial drake' and 'the mirror of the human soul'.

and white, as if a perpetual dusk is falling. *In the Heat of the Night* (2000) shows the duck shape in profile, described by the artist as 'derived from the ideal geometrical principle of the sphere'. Helnwein goes on to compare Donald Duck to the *Mona Lisa*: 'It is fascinating how this small drake so much better mirrors the human soul. In Donald we recognise our fears, our uncertainties and weaknesses – our stupidity, our vanity, our depravity, our jealousy and our simple-mindedness.'[14]

Finnish painter Kaj Stenvall's entire oeuvre involves Donald Duck. In *The Europeanized Drinking Habits* (2000), Donald is trapped inside a too-milky cup of coffee. His recent work pastiches familiar scenes or themes from well-known paintings and

Kaj Stenvall's *This is Not a Pipe*, 2002, points to Rene Magritte's 20th-century Surrealist series and our continuing 21st-century concerns with the real/not real.

popular culture. In *This is Not a Pipe* (2002) he touches the fake sky of the painted background behind him, a knowing, cynical art historian lecturing on the theme 'representing representation' or 'the suspension of disbelief', while the other hand theatrically gestures: 'See?'[15] In *Little Brother Sleeps, Big Brother Doesn't* (2000) he is tucked up snug between the glazed slices of an apple tart. We and Big Brother look down on the tasty snack. Thus we meet the real, the mass-produced and the soon to be dead duck in comic interplay.

Stooge or anti-hero, cartoon duck figures act out the political and philosophical concerns of the culture that produced them: a paper-thin world of violence enacted on/in animal life,

'Duck dipping' or hooking is a traditional game for children at fairgrounds, where rubber ducks bobbing along a channel of water are hooked up to win a prize.

of battery-run and animated toys, 'stolen' from the real. Animated ducks are submerged metaphors – small wonder Umberto Eco said he would talk about Donald Duck only in the presence of his analyst.

From Vaucanson to Stenvall by way of Pynchon, Disney, Lichtenstein and Takahashi, duck animation *performs* alienation from production by mass consumption, increasingly laying bare the device to ever more knowing audiences, yet reflecting nothing of depth, as if all we are aiming at is nothing more than a fairground duck, bobbing about on a moving surface. Device or toy, the ambiguity of duck at play is the subject of the next chapter.

5 Playing Duck

In Britain after the Second World War there was a fashion for the aspiring middle classes to have china ducks (usually mallard drakes) flying in a diagonal line up the wall of their living room. The ducks in a row have become a cultural icon of the British 1950s suburban interior, and now rate as collectable antiques. On the north-east coast of England, Whitby Lucky Ducks have been made in blown glass since the 1950s, in colours corresponding to gem stones associated with each month's birthday. Whitby Lucky Ducks have been credited with ending a drought in the South of France, boys being born to families with ('only') girls, financial winnings, success in exams or competitions and romantic engagements.

In parallel to the surplus of duck idiom, duck forms have multiplied with a vengeance for over 5,000 years. Duck-shaped objects exist today in disturbing quantities. For example, fine porcelain of the purest white has been made in Limoges, the china capital of France, since the mid-1800s. In Sarlat, the duck capital of France in the Périgord region, most of the produce is duck: the cafés and restaurants serve duck and duck souvenirs, include walking-sticks, condiment sets, cheese or cake slices, pots, jars, bottle openers, corkscrews, ashtrays, plates, cups, toilet roll and soap holders, bonbon dishes, cuddly toys, bath toys and plastic toys, hot-water bottle covers, towels, teacloths, place

Faience perfume vase in the form of a duck, Rhodes, c. 600–550 BC.

Cosmetic spoon representing a duck pulling a swimmer, 18th Dynasty (1801–1701 BC).

mats, serviettes, coasters, ornaments, trinkets, clocks, thermometers, coat-hooks, shoe brushes, baskets: all in the shape of ducks. Though superficially things of utility, the objects in Sarlat act in a kind of ecstatic consumerist duck orgy, a disturbing frenzy of duck tourism. Is this something duck have done to us, or we have done to duck? This tendency to over-ornament parallels what happens in language: not just extensive naming, but a kind of manic over-productivity, an effluence of duck trivia, where form cannot be restrained to function.

'The Big Duck', a building designed in the shape of a duck, on Long Island, New York, was built in 1930 by unemployed theatrical designers, with Model T tail-lights (which still work) and a wood-frame wire-mesh concrete surface, for a Depression-struck farmer to sell his duck meat and eggs in competition with the other 90 duck farms of his region. The Big Duck is now on the National Register of Historic Places, a 'building-becoming-sculpture', inspiring the architect Robert Venturi to coin the term 'duck' to describe when architecture is subordinate to the symbolic form.

Detail of a duck-spout on an Iron Age flagon found at Basse Yutz, France, c. 500 BC.

The Big Duck on Route 24, Long Island, a 'building-becoming-sculpture', or 'duck architecture'.

An easy alternative to the tortuously difficult-to-make origami duck: simply push out, fold and slot together.

As well as humans' compulsive relationship with their form, the duck can also play with perceptions. The Duck–Rabbit, 'arguably one of the most multistable images in modern psychology', obsessed the philosopher Ludwig Wittgenstein. Why? Wittgenstein writes about the 'seeing as' experience in visual puzzles such as Duck–Rabbit, where being both one and the other takes place only at the moment of seeing the change (such as from Duck to Rabbit). We do not see the duck *as* a rabbit but one or the other, as a kind of decoy to attract the mind. To see the duck becomes a language game, not of interpretation, but of perception.

'Duck dipping' or hooking is a traditional game for children at fairgrounds, where rubber ducks bobbing along a channel of water can be hooked up to win a prize. The Hobby-duck (a hobby-horse with a duck's head) in the Macclesfield Psalter of *c*. 1330 shows medieval art played for comedy as well as religious illumination. Duck playthings are as familiar as the animals themselves, from wooden wheeled ducks on sticks or cuddly toys

Wittgenstein's Duck–Rabbit puzzle: which do you see first?

Duck toys generally play on duck movement, especially the waddle.

for toddlers, to wind-up ducks, ornaments, trinkets and vehicles marketed for older children and adults. Konrad Lorenz demonstrated that ducks bond with 'toy' or sculpted objects, just as humans do. When a duck is effectively a pet it is tempting for humans to read this bond as a parallel emotional affection such as a child might feel towards a parent-figure, but the fact is, ducklings imprint on their first moving object, they follow any 'leader'.[1]

Designed to entertain in the flooded Red River delta, performed on village ponds or on the lake of a temple, the ancient art of *mua roi nuroc* (puppets that dance on water) has thrived in Vietnam since the eleventh century. The stage is the water's surface. Puppets dive underwater and reappear, worked by puppeteers who stand up to their waists in water, hidden from the audience by a bamboo or linen screen. They work their puppets on long bamboo poles submerged beneath the water, manipulating the arms and heads with hidden strings. Vietnamese water

Konrad Lorenz with a duck device to study 'imprinting', although a duck will actually follow anything or anyone.

puppetry has many mythical characters, but most abundant are those embodying ordinary peasants: fishermen and duck farmers. In one traditional plot known as 'Duck Catchers', an old couple carry a basket of eggs on stage which hatch into a flock of ducklings and the two try to tend to the lively little creatures. A fox hides in a tree, watching the ducklings. He pounces on one duckling and carries it off in his mouth, but the old couple chase the fox and beat him. Where the fox is invariably the trickster (as Jemima Puddleduck found to her cost), ducks are often the clowns in such performances.

The duck species familiar to Vietnamese farms and performance is the Indian runner duck (actually Indonesian). This

Indian runner duck Daphne in a tiara for the musical *Ducktastic,* allegedly stolen following a preview performance.

duck's salted meat and eggs were part of the diet aboard ships travelling from the East Indies in the 1500s. Live specimens were imported from India by the English by the 1830s, featured as 'penguin ducks' (because of their upright stature) in London Zoo in 1837 and thereafter came to be known as the 'Indian runner'. In the East Indies these ducks live a roving life in rice paddies where they feed on seeds, snails and insects. They are walked (or run) to the rice fields each morning behind a rag tied to the end of a pole, return at night to roost and lay, and eventually follow the same rag to market. As workers, pets or stars, Indian runner ducks are responsive to training, and often used for film and stage work. The comedy spectacular *Ducktastic*, briefly on stage in London's West End in 2005, featured Daphne the mind-reading duck, who early on in the show's run either escaped or was stolen. Since a dozen duck understudies (all of whom looked uncannily like one another) were waiting in the wings, this did not pose a problem, and the show went on, with its surreal sets of giant ducks laying gigantic eggs with singing, dancing and fooling actors inside.

There can be a dark side to this clowning, however. 'You expected hourglasses . . . you expected the skull-and-bones motif . . . You didn't expect the rubber duck. It was yellow.' In Terry Pratchett's *Soul Music*, from the Discworld series, Susan, granddaughter of Death (euphemistically called 'The Soul Cake Tuesday Duck'), visits his cottage. It is disturbingly clear to her that she has spent time there as a child. There is a rubber duck in the bathroom: uncontroversial proof. *Soul Music* is shot through with culturally specific duck jokes. University academics practising with bows and arrows shout 'Duck!' in the corridors, 'and among a group of tramps, the one they called the Duck man had a duck on his head. No one mentioned it. No one drew attention to it.' The man with a duck on his head is a metaphor for the book as a whole. As a drunk and a beggar, the Duck man is part of society's underclass or untouchables, invisible to mortals (as is Death). If the rubber duck's prosaic comic absurdity counters Death's sting, small wonder adults give every new baby a duck for the bath. But who invented this quack cure for mortality?

'One is never alone with a rubber duck', said Douglas Adams in *A Hitchhiker's Guide to the Galaxy* (1979). The exact history of the rubber duck and the identity of its inventor are not known, though it can be dated in relation to the development of the rubber manufacturing industry. After Brazilian waterproof gum rubber was 'discovered' by Columbus, it was used and experimented with in Europe and the US over the centuries leading to a 'rubber fever' in the 1830s. Charles Goodyear of tyres fame was an early industrialist who believed passionately in this new 'vegetable leather' or 'elastic metal'. For the Paris World Fairs of the 1850s he built pavilions entirely of rubber, floor to roof. Today there is a cultivated rubber tree for every two human beings on earth, but most 'rubber' ducks are now actually made of vinyl plastic. Therefore, a rubber duck is neither rubber nor a duck, but 'a vinyl plastic duckling toy'. Tell that to a two-year-old.

A rubber duck is also a term for a combat rubber raiding craft dropped from an aircraft with a parachute used by military groups to invade from sea quickly at times of war, adapted for times of peace or prosperity. The 'London Duck Tour' takes tourists in such a vehicle gaily painted yellow through the streets of the city, then, to everyone's delighted horror, rolls down a bank right into the waters of the River Thames, just like the toys dropped off bridges for duck charity races. These races are on an ever-increasingly large scale: on 24 November 2002 Singapore held its annual duck race, and the Singapore river turned yellow for a half-kilometre stretch as 123,500 rubber ducks vied to win the city-state's fifth annual Million Dollar Duck Race. Hundreds of spectators turned out to watch, and a record 1.2 million Singapore dollars was raised for various

A London Duck Tours bus, a converted DUKW (amphibious military truck), takes tourists on trips that include the River Thames.

Start of the Great British Duck charity race at Hampton Court in south-west London.

A few of the 165,000 ducks individually numbered for the Duck Race.

charities. This contest also achieved the world record for the largest number of ducks sponsored in a single competition. The owner of one of a few red ducks can win a million-dollar bonus. Later, the so-called celebrity ducks are auctioned off on the Internet to the highest bidder. Races involving little yellow rubber contestants are becoming increasingly popular worldwide, involving politicians and other human celebrities. The Great British Duck Race launched the largest ever number of rubber ducks – 165,000 – into the Thames at Hampton Court on 2 September 2007.

A 'Luxury' or designer rubber duck that mimics the colours of Pop art.

If you should want to, it is possible to collect any number of rubber ducks, of every size, style, colour and design. There are dead ducks (which float upside-down), camouflage, striped, Warhol-design, polka-dot ducks and even 'celebriducks' shaped to resemble icons of film, music, history or religion, such as Betty Boop, Elvis, Shakespeare and the Buddha. Clubs and online rubber duck forums such as 'duckplanet.com' exist on the Internet, where adult fans confess their passions and add to, sell and show their collections. Few of these ducks are for floating in the bath, obviously. There is a sense in which most toy or small ducks are collectable simply because they are 'cute': infantile, winsome, ironic, kitsch, with their big heads and eyes, open beaks, and round, rolling, waddling bodies, but the very surfeit evokes a certain unease: ours is a cultural embarrassment of rubber duckies.

'Luvvva Duck', a battery operated personal vibrating massager for women.

Yellow rubber ducks are generally for little naked human children to play with in the bath (when both species are arguably at their most 'natural' or innocent), though the 'personal vibrating massager' version called 'I rub my duckie' or 'Luvvva Duck' is described as 'A lady's best friend at bathtime', promoted as 'not intimidating to boyfriends or husbands'.

In 1988 the French artist Annette Messager produced *La Promesse des petites effigies* (*The Promise of Little Effigies*), in which children's toys such as teddy bears, pink elephants and yellow fluffy ducks were entombed in vertical glass cabinets hung with black and white photographs of body parts: lips, a laughing mouth, a foot, bottom, toes. Messager calls the toys 'the remains or little cadavers of childhood for which we stay very attached'. In 1999, for *Les Messagers de l'été* (*Messengers of Summer*), Messager used (real) stuffed animals given furry masks taken from cuddly toys, totally removing their natural or commercial cuteness, stripping them of their 'natural' dignity and giving them a macabre and threatening appearance. Human ridiculousness, producing cuddly toys in the shape of real animals or even stuffing dead animals as if alive, was unmasked. What is left of the *sauvage* once human animals – the 'man-made' – get their hands on it? The duck, wearing a furry mouse mask with green and pink ears, stood on the edge of a circled net, a smaller animal facing it. It looked freakish: genetically modified, or sinister – a toy bank robber or terrorist duck? Messager's duck toy differentiates between being animal in a state of nature with itself as a cultural being; wearing a social costume. The mask is at once human and non-human, duck and non-duck.

Given the variety of playthings in duck form, it is evident they are not merely cute representations of the animal, but highly suggestive commodities. They can be child or adult oriented, sexually naive or explicit, domestic, military, perceptual

Is Pokemon figure Psyduck prey to terrible headaches because of the unmanageable plethora of duckabilia?

or performative. The cute unmasks itself as its opposite; duck form follows function to the point of fable. A fable such as this: on 1 January 1994 a container ship ran into trouble in the Pacific Ocean, tumbling 29,000 plastic bath toys into the sea, 8,000 of which were ducks. After many years at sea, the world's biggest rubber duck flotilla has dispersed. Oceanographers and global warming scientists charting the flow of the currents are keen to know where they are being washed up. After drifting over 3,200 km (2,000 miles), hundreds beached in Alaska, with a number continuing through the Bering Strait into the Arctic, where the pack ice conveyed them over the North Pole into the North Atlantic Ocean. The most recent duck sighting was in Maine in July 2003, and pale versions of the yellow originals are expected to turn up along the Icelandic and British coasts any day now.[2]

These toy ducks have succeeded in a quest – for the fabled North-West Passage – where human sailors like Franklin and Nansen failed. Duck have drifted far from the wild into language itself, exemplifying the drift of meanings in metaphor. Though John Berger argued famously in 1973 that under the terms of capitalism, marginalization and commodification, 'the animal has been emptied of experience and secrets', he also admitted that 'sayings, dreams, games, stories, superstitions, language itself, recall them'.[3] And, more than for perhaps any other animal, this must be said of duck.

6 Quackery Unmask'd

In *The Character of a Quack-Doctor; or, The Abusive Practices of Impudent Illiterate Pretenders to Physick Exposed*, printed for Thomas Jones in 1676, the author rails against how quack doctors fly-post the streets with promises of wildly exaggerated cures: 'Such impudent ostentatious Decoy-papers he dayley spreads about the Streets, as if he had undertaken to serve the whole City with Bum-fodder, and plasters with his quackeries every Pissing-post, and therefore Lime-twigs the Rabble to become his Patients.'

Chapbooks and pamphlets, either advertising catalogues of cures and quack services or warning against their dangers, were familiar parts of European street reading from the fifteenth century to the nineteenth, and satiric verses, plays and musicals also featured quacks.[1] The derogatory (highly metaphoric) language describe them as 'cheats, imposters, piss-artists and jugglers in urinals' (logically enough, since disease and infection show up in urine), their 'decoy-papers' offered as lures to a gullible public as decoys are to unsuspecting ducks *Quackery Unmasked: A Treatise on Venereal Disease* slates 'Those Fools and Knaves' who offer questionable cures for a vast range of disorders (colds, wrinkles, toothache, earache, deafness, scurvy, fever, the pox, madness, shyness, a low forehead, tumours, gall and kidney stones, loss of virginity and so on) with 'feel-good'

Quackery Unmask'd:

OR,

REFLECTIONS

On the SIXTH EDITION of Mr. *MARTIN*'s Treatife of the VENEREAL DISEASE, and its APPENDIX;

And the PAMPHLET call'd,

The Charitable Surgeon, &c.

CONTAINING

A Full and Plain Detection and Refutation of fome grofs *Errors*, &c. of thofe Authors: Interfpers'd with many new and ufeful *Obfervations* concerning the *Venereal Difeafe*; and the *Method* and *Medicines* proper for its *fpeedy*, *fafe*, and *effectual Curation*. Proper Remarks on Mr. *Martin*'s *Admirable Medicine*, and his *Infallible Prefervative*. A Full and True Account of *Quacks*; and their *Method of Practice*. An Account of fome *Excellent Medicines*, &c.

Highly neceffary to be read by all *Venereal Patients*, who would prevent their own *Ruin*; and by all *Phyficians*, *Surgeons*, and *Apothecaries*, who are here Vindicated from Mr. *Martin*'s *Afperfions*.

By *J. SPINKE*, Licens'd Practitioner in Phyfick and Surgery.

LONDON: Printed, and Sold by *D. Brown*, without *Temple-Bar*, *G. Strahan*, at the *Golden-Ball* in *Cornhill*, *J. Woodward* in St. *Chriftopher*'s Church-Yard, in *Threadneedle-ftreet*, *B. Barker*, at the *White-Hart*, in *Weftminfter-Hall*; and the Author at his Houfe, the *Golden-Ball*, between the *Sun* and *Caftle Taverns* in *Honey-Lane Market*, *Cheapfide*. Price 1 s. 6 1709.

remedies often simply high in alcohol.[2] *Dottore*, a stock *commedia
dell'arte* caricature of gluttony and pedantic learning, is sometimes depicted with a mask like a duck's beak. *Dottore* blathers
on and on in fake Latin and shown up as a quack by the end of
the play.

Though quacks were regarded as profiteers, they alone had
the gall to treat conditions that registered physicians would not
risk, often operating in the street, then and there. Barber surgeons amalgamated in 1504 in London to form an elite company, but surgery was not established as a respectable profession
until 1800, and recognized surgeons and doctors had their rep-
utations and high prices to protect. Master-quack James
Graham, working between 1745 and 1794, whose speciality was
'electrical treatments and frictions', invented an extraordinary

An oiled-cloth mask with a bronze beak, thought to keep infections at bay, used by 18th-century plague doctors in Venice.

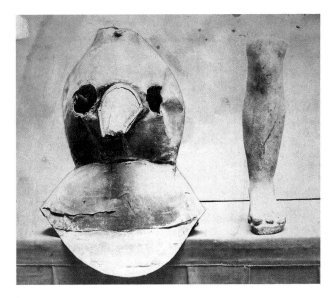

test of public credulity with his 'Celestial Magnetico-Electrico Bed', said to have cost Graham £10,000 to make.[3] One night on the vibrating mattress made of stallion's hair would apparently cure any couple of infertility, for the princely sum of £50. Quacks have always been chancers, like those flooding the Internet with spam cures for physical and sexual disorders less imaginatively today.

The term 'quack', a pretender to medical skill, or dishonest person, may derive from early Dutch *kwakzalver*, hawker of salve, or the German *Quacksalber*, a questionable salesperson. According to German–English idiomatic history, to quack meant to shout in the Middle Ages (as quacksalvers sold market wares by shouting in a loud voice). Due to the similarity to the German word for mercury or 'quicksilver', *Queckzilber*, myths have arisen about quack dentists and doctors performing the

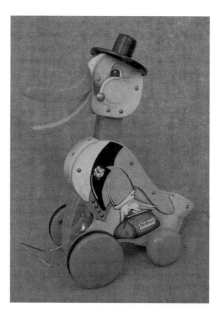

Quack Doctor toy 'Dr Duck' has an open beak for 'quacken' (bragging) and a breast for 'quackery' (money for bogus medicines).

first fillings and mercury cures for syphilis. For the Dutch, *quackery* is still bogus money-making medical practices and *quacken* is to brag. Slovak for a quack is *sarlatan* (a charlatan), and the Vietnamese still have a phrase for 'quackish', *co tinh chat lang bam*.

The quack doctor parallels the traits of the duck: over-determined figures of plenitude and perpetual buoyancy, noisy, unreliable, playfully comic in the face of sober subjects such as health, greed, sex and death. This final chapter examines the duck's chaotic hybridity via the life-and-death issues of the avian flu virus, extinct and threatened species, hybrid or 'misfit' duck figures and, finally, how it is that duck contributes to holding up the world.

A puddle-duck meets a harsher, more realistic end in Ernest Griset's 1880s illustration.

You will get ti de'eath o' cold,
Then we shall ha' to bury thee,
Then t' worms'll come an ate thee up,
Then t' ducks'll come an ate t' worms,
Then we shall go an' ate th' ducks,
On Ilkla Moor bath 'at.

If Death is the remedy all singers dream of, duck songs are no exception. Should you be foolish enough to go on 'Ilkla Moor baht at' (on Ilkley Moor, Yorkshire, without a hat) you'll die of the cold, waste in the ground, feed worms which the ducks eat and the dialect song ends: 'then we shall go an' ate th' ducks'. This is our shared animal hunter–hunted death–life cycle, as sung by Lewis Carroll's Manlet: 'Where the Frog is pursued by the Duck;/ Where the Ducklet is chased by the Doglet–/ So runs the world's luck!'[4]

La Cane
De Jeanne
Est morte d'avoir fait
Du moins on le presume
Un rhume
Mauvais!

'La Cane de Jeanne', by singer, poet and 'grand anarchist' Georges Bresson. A duck, found dead over her egg, her chick unhatched, leaves no widower – so we unfeelingly inherit her feathers and egg. 'La Cane de Jeanne has died', so Bresson prophetically presumed, of 'un rhume / Mauvais', a bad cold. Avian flu, perhaps?

There have been a number of significant pandemics in human history, often 'zoonoses' (infectious diseases transmitted from animals to humans) that came about with the domestication of animals. Spanish flu (an HINI virus of 1918–19), which killed 25 million people in six months, is now thought to have originated in birds. Migratory waterfowl are the natural reservoir of the avian influenza virus, particularly wild ducks. Avian flu first appeared in 1997, since then evolving into several strains. Scientists are increasingly worried that its deadliest strains (HPAI and H5NI), if combined with the human flu virus in what is called a 'reassortment' of the genes, will prove exceptionally dangerous, and could even be the next pandemic, killing millions of people. Virologists agree H5NI presents a risk, and while some governments have stockpiled influenza drugs, it is currently a threat without a vaccine. Foods high in sialic acid may help prevent the illness, and the only currently available drug to combat the virus is Tamiflu, patented and produced by a giant Swiss pharmaceutical company, which has stated that it will need years to stockpile enough drugs to deal

A ringed eider hen is checked in Tutakoke Bird Camp, Hooper Bay, Alaska, as part of the Avian Influenza Sampling Project, 2006.

with a pandemic. In response to global anxiety millions of birds are being and will be killed: ducks in particular, since they can carry and excrete high levels of this highly pathogenic virus without seeming ill.

The wetlands of the Danube delta are a major migratory area for wild duck from Europe and Africa: after tests on ducks from this region in 2004 revealed the virus in duck faeces, the European Union banned all poultry from Romania and Turkey. In 2005 scientists urgently called nations to prepare for a global influenza pandemic that could strike 20 per cent of the world's population, and in the same year the Thai government culled three million free-range ducks. Birds found infected with the strain range from pintail ducks tested in Alaska to birds on Lake Pinghai in China; recent scares in Kazakhstan, Mongolia and Siberia have all been attributed to H5N1. Most sinister is that, since ducks do not typically become ill when infected, the virus may be present in pets, food or water, and (this is probably what whips up human hysteria) duck can fly anywhere, all over the world, impervious to borders. There is increasing evidence that a thriving international trade in smuggled poultry – including live birds, chicks and meat – is helping spread bird flu.[5] Poultry smuggling, especially intensive between China and Africa, is a huge business that poses a unique threat since the A(H5NI) – the A virus causes influenza in birds and humans – bird flu virus is robust enough to survive not just in live birds but also in frozen meat, feathers, bones and even on cages, though it dies with cooking. Duck flu is a virus with potential, like the chain of associations in imagery.

Despite sensational media reporting, though complacency must be avoided, avian flu cannot be categorized as a pandemic because the virus cannot yet cause human–human transmission. Confirmed human cases reported to the WHO in June 2008 of avian influenza A(H5NI) comprise 385 cases of infection and 243 deaths. Of the deaths 110 were in Indonesia and 52 in Vietnam. The pattern of pandemics since the Black Death and Asiatic or Spanish flu suggest parallels can be drawn which may feed racist fears of uncontrolled migrating animals and disease coming from the East.

Whatever the outcome of avian flu, ducks have already given up their lives to humans in what must be trillions over the centuries. Some are already extinct; many more are threatened. Ducks have been with us for 50 million years, but how many species will survive as long again? Over-hunting, loss of habitat via deforestation and the draining of marshlands (often for human property development and tourism) combine to threaten the West Indian black-billed whistling duck, the Australian freckled duck, the white-headed Spanish duck, eider duck, the Baikal teal of Japan and Korea, the Brazilian merganser and the marbled teal in Iraq. Gunshot and fishing sinkers give ducks lead poisoning. The torrent duck's specialized habitat requirements – clear, swiftly flowing waters – are easily destroyed by river pollution; the harlequin duck population has declined since the *Exxon Valdez* oil spill in 1989. As the water table becomes

Duck are especially vulnerable to oil spills and polluted water.

Duck skins with expedition labels.

increasingly polluted more living creatures and plants become affected, and waterfowl are among the first to suffer.

'It is a sad fact that as soon as a species declines to rarity, the demand for museum skins increases.'[6] It is now thought that the tragically ironic reason for the Auckland Island merganser's extinction may well have been the number shot by museum collectors in 1901. The last pair, shot on 9 January 1902, are skeletons in the Natural History Museum at Tring in England. Baron Walter Rothschild's formerly private zoological museum at Tring houses a collection he started at the age of seven, and opened to the public in 1892. As part of the biggest bird collection in the world, Tring has two million skeletons, spirit, egg and nest specimens and 'skins' (a body stuffed flat with wood wool or shavings for research purposes rather than display) donated by collectors from 1800 to the present. There are thousands of duck specimens, each labelled with the collector, place and date of collection, stored in sliding drawers on flat trays, in floor to ceiling filing.

But in many cases the collection ends in the 1950s. With no funds to pay collectors for new specimens, and few amateur naturalists, zoologists or ornithologists who know where to send a dead duck for study, only five curators remain at Tring. Technological progress may have been most active from the 1960s to the present, but surely it is a cultural disaster to have no specimens available for the study of the effects of hybridity, pollution or global warming?

Sadly, the extinction of a few duck species is unlikely to make international news or bother the general public. The fact that ducks seem as ubiquitous as humans or houseflies inures us to the risks they are vulnerable to. Rats, weasels, mink, badgers, raccoons, squirrels and skunks steal duck eggs; coyotes, turtles, hawks and large fish eat ducklings; dogs, big cats, birds of prey and foxes eat adult duck; but none of this comes close to the scale of human predation. The greatest hazard is duck sociability. Ducks are highly vulnerable to netting and shooting, or baiting with poisoned grain. Large gatherings can do enormous damage eating newly sown crops, ripening cereals, grasslands, rape or fodder grass, trampling soil, or spoiling fields with so many droppings that other animals will not graze. Farmers can reduce cereal crops, offer lure crops or bait stations, use acoustic devices (gas cannons, pistols), visual scares (flags, sacks, wires, scarecrows) or, more radically, toxic fertilizer or hunt and kill the ducks.[7] If not compensated for their loss, farmers 'can make

Disappearing wetland causes habitat problems for duck, but before and after shots of drained farmland followed by wetland restoration are optimistic.

life as inhospitable as possible for waterfowl. Feelings ran so strongly in the 1950s in Saskatchewan, Canada, there were marches on the Legislative Building to treat mallard duck as vermin with a bounty paid for killing them.'[8]

Yet humans are also aware of the need to make room for ducks. Forward-thinking architect Cedric Price made plans for turning redundant Hamburg Docks into a 'Ducklands' bird sanctuary. From the duck perspective, much of the land currently being returned to waterfowl was originally *their* wetlands and prairies, now prey to agricultural expansion, with progressive soil and water degradation. Increasingly, 'natural' farmers or gardeners (such as Britain's Prince Charles) imitate the inexpensive organic methods of less-developed parts of the world,

using ducks to control insect populations on their crops rather than pesticides. Adaptation and hybridity are duck's specialities. The common mallard (*Anas platyrhynchos*) is one of the oldest ducks classified (by Linnaeus himself in 1758) and the most familiar and widespread across the world, numbering more than 10 million birds. Its status is thought to be secure, with as many domesticated as feral on the planet. A duck is labelled 'feral' when carrying duck plague or the flu virus, when force-copulating out of its usual group or tribe (affecting indigenous duck populations, causing cross-breeds and hybrids), in other words, when 'out of control' and requiring culling, isolation or other 'humane management'. Yet, constructing the idea of a feral duck is itself a metaphor.

If human tourism threatens ducks, duck tourism is as controversial in its turn, as the ruddy duck controversy discussed earlier illustrates. The latest research argues that since the ruddy duck was introduced artificially into Europe, it is justified to cull those birds, unlike in North America, where they are

With the right wetland habitats, we may again have 'skies black with duck' such as those Charles Dickens saw in the USA.

indigenous.[9] But they can easily fly over the Atlantic. What is the threat? Does inter-breeding weaken or invigorate? As one 'pure' breed loses distinctive aspects of its genetic makeup and culture, new formations arise. The campaigning case against the cull is that it is not a control programme but a senseless massacre, 'killing in the name of blood purity . . . dangerously retrograde . . . as Nature is not pure. Nature is not fixed. It is flux.' The real fear is that such stories are distracting ornithologists from the far more important issues of 'confronting powerful industrial and agricultural interests whose land development and polluting activities are responsible for the decimation of any number of species',[10] but the ruddy duck story is a good example of how trivialization and hyperbole are as central parts of duck narratives (ruddy 'lager louts', 'a plague of hybrids', etc.) as they enter our culture via the tabloid press and popular campaigns as well as academic studies. You simply cannot rarefy duck stories; they will always duck out of seriousness into humour or word play.

Hybridity is part of domestication (muscovy and mallard hybrids 'mulards' are more efficient food converters, for example) and natural behaviour in the wild (pochard mate with scaup, mallard with wigeon or gadwall, etc.). As global movement increases, so do hybrid species, clustering in different regions of the world. If the white-headed duck's exaggerated bill evolves into the knowing smile of the red-headed ruddy duck, this will be a fact of life: hybridity is both symptom of and healthy resistance to duck imperialism, creating new transcultural forms. Duck is part of an unstable story of quacks, misfits and migrations, cruel or cheerful expediency, and it is work ostensibly for children that best expresses this.

Hans Christian Andersen's *The Ugly Duckling* (1844) is generally considered a metaphor for his own life. Tall and gawky,

awkward in company but longing to fit in, Andersen can be seen as his own ugly duckling, teased and jeered at, a perpetual outsider.

> The duckling was quite melancholy because he was so desperately ugly and because he was the laughing-stock of the whole duck-yard . . . even his mother said: 'How I wish you were miles away.' [Seasons pass and the ugly

duckling, who has been hiding in the marshes away from the cruelty of his life, takes to the lake.] But what did he see there? He beheld its own image and it was no longer the reflection of a clumsy, dirty, grey bird, ugly offensive. He himself was a swan! Being born in a duck-yard does not matter, if only you are hatched from a swan's egg.[11]

Another ugly duckling was the Victorian poet, painter and misfit Edward Lear, whose nonsense songs – many of which he put to music and sang to the piano, somewhere between laughter and sobbing – typically relate stories of travel and adventure by unlikely but devoted couples. A Nutcracker runs away with the Sugartongs, an Owl with a Pussycat, and a Duck with a Kangaroo. The desire for release from the mundane world ('my life is a bore on this nasty pond,/ and I long to go out in the world beyond!') sees escape into the unfamiliar as a joy ('and we'd go to the Dee and the Jelly Bo Lee/Over the land and over the sea'). But the greatest reason for going is love ('All to following my own dear true / Love of a Kangaroo?'), just as Lear himself was happiest when travelling with his lifelong friend and unrequited love, Franklin Lushington. It is not just Lear's loneliness, epilepsy, depression and longing for love that make the songs so melancholic, it is the deliberate emphasis placed on vulnerable absurdity. If the duck went alone, it could easily fly: if it loved another duck, they would simply migrate together. But biological determinism does not create good literature, nor is life always this simple. For rich metaphors of the mind, 'semantics needs impossible worlds'.[12] The duck chooses to love outside its own species. This makes the going more difficult, but the comparative pleasures the greater, perhaps: 'And who was so happy, – O who? / As the Duck and the Kangaroo?' A stable future for ducks is as precarious as Lear pictures it.

Victorian poet and artist Edward Lear's unlikely pairing of Duck and Kangaroo, who travel the world together.

Duck operates comfortably in the fields of cartoon, picture-book and nonsense verse, but why is there no ode to a duck? F. W. Harvey's poem may do for one:

From troubles of the world I turn to ducks,
Beautiful comical things . . .[13]

Mandarin Ducks, a film installation by Jeroen de Rijke and Willem de Rooj, representing the Netherlands for the 51st Venice Biennale in 2005, is a similarly enigmatic title: ten people meet in a flat one Sunday afternoon, talk of chaos, love, corruption, consumption, ideals, and work, intercut with reference to theatre, sitcom and mainstream film language. It reads like finding 87 eggs in one duck's nest. Like ducks, the people are noisy and ultimately 'full of sound and fury,/ Signifying nothing'.[14] Languages – like all animals including people – are hybrids. The life of ducks is like that of the 'mongrel tongue' of English ('a gallimaufry or hodgepodge of all other speeches', said Edmund Spenser in 1579);[15] what we call English is a mix of

Celtic, Gaelic, Latin, Greek, Anglo-Saxon, Jute, Norse, Scandinavian, French and many other languages.

The duck's natural history revealed its sociability and adaptability as eminently suitable for modern hybridity. The word 'pressed' '(the being-pressed, the being-with as being strictly attached, bound, enchained, being under pressure, compressed, impressed, repressed, pressed-against . . .)' is prescient to understanding duck. Hence the oppressed Farmer Duck begins a revolution which overthrows the fat farmer for a collective, animal farm. Take the 'compression' of verbal diarrhoea in duck idiom, or how 'impressed', 'repressed' misfits perform alienation from production like Disney's duck, also found in Lear's nonsense verse or Hans Christian Andersen's fairy tale. In the field of naming-as-dominion, the biblical book of Genesis has God allowing Adam or Ish to name the animals, which 'represents at the same time his sovereignty and his loneliness'.[16] If the over-productivity of language and cultural artefacts (as examined in chapters on the duck's sound and form) is a symptom of our loneliness, the duck is the palliative – as delivered by a quack-doctor – a metaphor for 'being-together', like all the eider on the planet massing in the same place in the Arctic. Because duck can use the skies and seas, they can gather in one huge 'mobile vulgus'[17] – Elias Canetti's term for the moveable and excitable crowd – in numbers we landlocked humans cannot. Perhaps this is why the duck is such an abundant motif for us: we share its need for the reassuring sound and company of others.

If anthropomorphism is the remains of continuous use of animal metaphor, do we still see the duck 'out there' in the skies and on the waters with its own reality, or have we claimed duck as an imaginary friend?[18] If we balk at the facts, if facts fail us, metaphor remains a way of supposing: it brings insight into the confusion of existence by transferring what we do not know to

Almost anything in the world can be refashioned as a duck.

160

The eponymous 'Farmer Duck' works like a dog before the farm animals overthrow the oppressor in Martin Waddell's and Helen Oxenbury's *Animal Farm*-inspired *Farmer Duck* (1991) for five-year-olds.

The duck brought the sheep from the hill.

"How goes the work?" called the farmer.

The duck answered,

"Quack!"

things we do know; the less familiar to the more. 'Reality is a cliché from which we escape by metaphor.'[19] In the face of reality's heavyweight pressures, humans create new realities, and our best duck metaphors are a sign of some new disclosure, a living 'stream of semiosis': Duck metaphors can be cute (as with cuddly or rubber ducks), can be ornament (tiles or flying ducks), can become a household cliché (toilet-duck), anthropomorphically act out phonic jokes (Duck in a Truck), sign (quack and waddle) or perform the real and ideal (from Vaucanson's to the mechanical tin duck), to name just a few. The possibilities are endless.

This is not just naming or labelling duck but providing metaphors for over-productivity. The superabundance of duck

Gods with duck heads, a magical engraved gem or amulet, 3rd–4th century AD, chalcedony.

'things' – dictionaries crammed with duck words, cupboards overflowing with duck trinkets, duck in culture all around us – works as metaphor for the exuberance of the creature but also as a set of man-made decoys for keeping the real duck figurative. Whilst the commercialized market (rubber ducks) utilizes clichéd duck metaphor, avant-garde duck material (picturebooks, cartoon, music, sound and art work) struggles to express the cultural risks felt with the loss of a shared notion of a real duck. Is the species chased, pressed and over-domesticated to extinction, 'irredeemable for the culture of capitalism'?[20] Lord love a duck, let's hope not. Yet how could it be? We use duck in so many aspects of our lives. Duck proliferates all culture and all modes of culture: a production of our post-colonial, post-modern, post-industrial world, the effluence of duck trivia part of our manic over-productivity, a figure of flux and contradictory value.

Early attempts at classification struggled with how on earth this creature could be equally at ease on land, air or water, yet 'sometimes above and sometimes under' is the continuing mystery of the duck. Duck is an animal for science and myth with characteristics and observable behaviours, but it is also uniquely close to human subjectivity as a toy, pet or meal. Duck is expressive of the gods, the elements, cosmic life and death, whilst in everyday reality it behaves as variously and badly as humans. Yet this special relation we have with the species 'that form a collective multiplicity, a becoming', as philosophers Gilles Deleuze and Félix Guattari put it,[21] will be lost if only their 'cuteness' wins. We know duck; they are as silly as we are. They are obvious metaphors for us. But duck are also real. The legend of Amala, mythological giant of the Tsimshian Native Americans,[22] carries a final important warning: Amala holds up the earth on a spinning pole behind his back and must balance it. Once a year a servant applies duck oil to his back muscles to relieve him. The Tsimshian believe once all the ducks have been hunted to extinction, the servant will not come to apply duck oil and the world will fall from the pole and be destroyed.

A basalt statue of Ehecatl-Quetzalcoatl, Aztec god of the wind, wearing a duck's beak mask, c. 1324–1521.

In the Preface to this book legends described how duck made the world; now we see how duck sustains it. The Tsimshian legend describes the crucial value of duck, not as animal celebrity or revered totem, but a seemingly ordinary, jolly little animal whose *production* holds up our world. We depend on it bobbing back up as tireless metaphor for buoyant survival in the face of human exploitation. We can study duck and never know its diversity, have it close to us wild, tamed or cute, wear it for warmth, sleep under it, write with it, eat it, speak it, play with it. It serves our pleasure. However much we take the cheery, watery little creature for granted, duck is the finest *use-metaphor* on the planet, and lord love a duck for that.

> Be kind to your web-footed friend,
> For a duck may be somebody's mother,
> Be kind to your friends in the swamp
> Where the weather is cold and damp –
> You may think that this is the end,
> Well, it is.[23]

'Fantastic! *And* it was all written with a feather!'[24]

Timeline of the Duck

80–50 million BC	15000–8000 BC	3000–2000 BC	1500 BC	c. 1350 BC
Fossils suggest ducks lived with dinosaurs and survived whatever wiped out the dinosaurs	Prehistoric Solutrean cave paintings at Tajo de las Figuras by peoples from North Africa using natural ochre pigments show duck were hunted and classified	Bronze Age and Iraq duck weights indicate duck for trade	Indian religious text *Rig-Veda* describes a duck that lays golden eggs on a nest built on the head of a thief	Egyptian scenes *Fowling in the Marshes* and Bronze Age artefacts like *The Zsujta Duck* and *Cart Fitting* indicate duck is systematically trapped, hunted and domesticated by humans

c. AD 1000	1187	1605	c. 1650	c. 1660s
American Indian canvasback decoys made of tule rush reeds	Gerald of Wales, *Topographia Hibernia*, describes duck as forming on trees and dropping off either into the water or on land	The barnacle goose, described as a vegetable, can be roasted and eaten for Lent by priests	Duck decoys built by Dutch engineers in Europe	Metsu's *The Sleeping Sportsman* pictures the consonance between duck hunting and sex

1910	1937	1948	c. 1950	c. 1960
Fabre's 'Le Canard' biplane flies 500 m over water	Disney's Donald Duck features in a cartoon for the first time	Citroen 2cv invented, to enable two peasants to drive 100 kg of farm goods to market at 60 km/h, in clogs and across muddy unpaved roads. It uses no more than 3 litres of petrol to travel 100 km. Famously, it is able to drive across a ploughed field without breaking any eggs	The McCarthyism 'If it looks like a duck and quacks like a duck' becomes part of anti-Communist crusade	Chuck Berry makes the 'Duck Walk' or 'Duck Dance' famous

300–250 BC	AD 500–800	c. AD 650	AD 960–1127
Tanagra, Greece *Faience vessel in the form of 'Eros Riding a Duck'*	Bolas weapons used to throw into flocks of wild duck 	St Cuthbert, Celtic monk, Prior at Lindisfarne, keeps an eider duck, as shown in stained-glass window in Great Salkeld church, Cumbria	Peking duck was the court dish of the Northern Song Dynasty

1676	1739	c. 1850	1892
A taxonomic history of the Anatidae begins in English with Willughby and Ray's classification of aquatic birds	Vaucanson exhibits his robot duck for the first time in Paris Salons: it becomes the toast of Europe	English Aylesbury ducks at the height of their reputation as 'the tastiest in the country'	Tring Zoological museum and library opened to the public

1984	1991	1997	1998	2005
George Orwell invents 'duckspeak' in his novel *1984*	Martin Waddell and Helen Oxenbury produce the picture-book *Farmer Duck*	First recorded instance of human infection with H5N1, avian flu	Out of 29,000 bath-toys, 8,000 rubber ducks fall out of a container ship and are lost at sea	The i-duck flash-memory storing device for computers is invented

References

PREFACE

1 Giraldus Cambrensis, *Topographia Hibernia* [1187]; as Gerald of Wales, *The History and Topography of Ireland* (Harmondsworth, 1951), p. 41.
2 Ibid.
3 Sacred song attributed to Alain de Lille (1128–1202), theologian and poet.

1 NATURAL HISTORY

1 The tribal arrangement was first proposed by Jean Delacour and Ernst Mayr in 1945, and developed by Paul A. Johnsgard from 1961.
2 B. Grzimek et al., eds, *Grzimek's Animal Life Encyclopedia*, 2nd edn (New York, 2003).
3 'Cretaceous duck ruffles feathers', BBC News: news.bbc.co.uk/1/hi/sci/tech/4187287.stm (accessed January 2005).
4 Descriptive observations from John C. Phillips, *A Natural History of the Ducks*, 4 vols (Boston, MA, 1922–6).
5 Though the 'demon duck of doom' or giant dinosaur duck from the late Miocene period is popularly described as a 3m high carnivorous duck with a bill the size and shape of an axe, it is – by its surmised appearance – as likely to be related to the emu (BBC News: news.bbc.co.uk/1/hi/world/asia-pacific/ 5172292.stm (accessed September 2000).
6 Jean-Claude Fischer, 'Oiseaux', in *Guide des fossiles de France* (Paris, 2000), p. 183.

7 Phillips, *A Natural History of the Ducks*, vol. I, p. 8.

8 C. Eykman, *The European Anatidae: An Easy Method of Identifying Swans, Geese and Ducks* (Amsterdam, 1930).

9 Stolzman (1886); quoted in Phillips, *A Natural History of the Ducks*, vol. IV, p. 224.

10 T. C. Eyron, *A Monograph of the Anatidae or Duck Tribe* (London, 1838).

11 'A Frog He Would a Wooing Go'. A 'rowley-powley' is a plump fowl.

12 Great Salkeld is a tiny English village in the Eden Valley close to the Lake District, its church first built in 880, one of 40 marking the resting places of the body of St Cuthbert, carried from Holy Island by monks fleeing the invading Danes. On the south side of the nave is a memorial window, which shows St Cuthbert in his cell on Farne Island with an eider duck by his side. The same eider duck, or 'Cuddy's duck', features in the tapestry worked by the women of Great Salkeld to commemorate the 1300th anniversary of the death of St Cuthbert. The saint, shown seated with the duck on his lap, is surrounded by scenes of village life and labour, and by panels representing the four seasons.

13 Cited in Mark L. Mallory et al., 'Unusual Migration Mortality of King Eiders', *Waterbirds: The International Journal of Waterbird Biology*, XXIV/3 (December 2001), p. 453.

14 Cited in Phillips, *A Natural History of the Ducks*, vol. I, p. 65.

15 A. E. Brehm, quoted in ibid., p. 123.

16 Phillips suggests 'an astonishing locality for Tree ducks is Lake Junin, Peru, altitude over 11,000 feet where in April 1920, Lord William Percy shot a single specimen and saw at least a dozen others' (*A Natural History of the Ducks*, vol. I, p. 130).

17 Ibid., vol. IV, pp. 164–75.

18 Ibid.

19 David Tomlinson, *Ducks* (London, 1996), p. 12.

20 Ibid.

21 Paul Johnsgard, *Ducks, Geese and Swans of the World* (London, 1978), p. 384.

22 Ibid.

23 Patrick Sawyer, 'Love a Duck', *Evening Standard* (7 February 2005).

24 K. McCracken, 'The 20-cm Spiny Penis of the Argentina Lake Duck (oxyura vittata)', *The Auk*, 117/3 (2000), pp. 820–25.

25 Hudson cited in Phillips, *A Natural History of the Ducks*, vol. I, p. 31.

26 Crawshay cited in ibid., vol. II, p. 207.

27 Cited in ibid., vol. I, p. 34.

28 T. Grandin and C. Johnson, *Animals in Translation* (London, 2006), pp. 69–71. J. Gellatley, *Ducks out of Water: A Report on the UK Duck Industry* by VIVA (Vegetarians International Voice for Animals) in 2006 records ducks kept 10,000 at a time in darkness without access to water, requiring debeaking and antibiotics against the behaviours and disease that factory farm conditions exacerbate. VIVA is lobbying for legal regulations rather than UK 'codes'.

29 The 'Ig Nobel' prize, awarded in Harvard since 1991, is given to published research findings that make the panel laugh; for 'achievements that cannot or should not be reproduced' (www.improbable.com).

30 B. Bagemihl, *Biological Exuberance: Animal Homosexuality and Natural Diversity* (New York, 1999), p. 494.

2 THE FREE AND THE PRESSED

1 Colin Willcock, *Duck Shooting* (London, 1962).

2 E. G. Bolen, 'Waterfowl Management: Today and Tomorrow', *Journal of Wildlife Management*, LXIV/2 (April 2000), pp. 323–35.

3 Coffin text 62, trans. J. Affman: www.nefertiti.iwebland.com/timelines/topics/fishing_and_hunting.htm (accessed 2007).

4 The bolas in Exeter Museum was collected by the Reverend J. Dyson, who sailed around the world from 1885 to 1889. References to natives kayaking out to ships ready to trade artefacts – which may have been made expressly for trading – can be found in the journals of First Lieutenant George Peard, sent on a mission of exploration in the years 1825–8 to the Pacific Ocean and Bering Strait. See also J. R. Bockstoce, *Eskimos of N. W. Alaska in the Early Nineteenth Century* (Oxford, 1977).

5 Mid-twentieth-century dance crazes such as 'Do the Duck' and Chuck Berry's 'Duck Walk' may derive from these indigenous hunting-related duck dances.

6 Vincent Giannetto III, hunter-carver, has made his living solely as a decoy carver for more than 25 years, according to *Wildfowling* magazine. He began making his own as a teenager, when he couldn't afford to buy decoys – now his 'Delaware River style gunning decoys', each 'unique in look, feel, position and character', are worth thousands of dollars, and have appeared in the Smithsonian Institute and museum exhibitions. Gianetto has been invited to the White House to honour his craftsmanship.

7 A. L. Kroeber and R. H. Lowie, eds, *American Archaeology and Ethnology*, vol. XXV (Los Angeles, 1929).

8 Lewis Clement, 'Duck Decoying in France [in the Abbeville marshes near Amiens]', *Baily's Magazine* (January 1874), pp. 351–7.

9 L. Budgen, *Songs from Lewis Carroll's Sylvie and Bruno* (London, 1899), and Frank L. Baum, *Mother Goose in Prose* (London, 1899).

10 Nikolai Mikhailovich Przhevalsky, *From Kulja, Across the Tian Shan to Lob-Nor*, trans. E. D. Morgan (London, 1878).

11 'Bird Hunting in Mexico', birdhuntingmexico.com/ duck_hunting.aspx (accessed 23 July 2007).

12 John G. Mackenty, *Duck Hunting* (London, 1964), p. 150.

13 Retold in 1904 by Yakumo Koizumi (Lafcadio Hearn) in *Kwaidan: Stories and Studies of Strange Things*, trans. T. Takata (London, 1933).

14 The shadow play featured in OBON: *Tales of Rain and Moonlight*, multi-media performance, directed by Ping Chong & Company (Tokyo, 2003).

15 In a chapter titled 'A Series of Damn Fool Things' from *Duck Hunting*, Mackenty deplores lit cigarettes, walking on thin ice, leaving the safety catch off guns and wearing waders that can fill with water and drown the wearer in marshes, rivers or the sea.

16 Isabel Colegate, *The Shooting Party* (London, 1980), p. 17.

17 E. de Jongh, 'Erotica in Vogelperspectief', Digitale Biblioteck voor de Nederlandse Letteren, www.dbnl.org/tekst/jong.htm, p. 21 (accessed 2007).

18 'Domesticated' implies duck's genetic make-up (thus gene pool) having been altered to satisfy the needs of humans such that if the animal is placed back into its natural environment, it will be at a selective disadvantage when competing against its wild counterparts.

19 Juliet Clutton-Brook, ed., *The Walking Larder: Patterns of Domestication, Pastoralism and Predation* (London, 1989), p. 22: Sandor Bökönyi's definition.

20 Diodorus of Sicily, *The Library of History* [1968], trans. C. B. Welles, 12 vols (London, 1933), Chapter 60.

21 Sytze Bottema, 'Modern Domestication Processes', in Clutton-Brook, ed., *The Walking Larder*, p. 40.

22 Robert Gibbs, *A History of Aylesbury* (Aylesbury, 1855), p. 622.

23 W. Ranger, *Report to the General Board of Health* (London, 1849), p. 5.

24 W. Rose, *Fifty Years Ago*, Little Booklets on Haddenham Village (Northumberland, 1931), pp. 24–5.

25 Aylesbury ducks were a well-known export to London where Potter's family were based, and after a lifetime of animal interest, Potter was later to breed and show farm animals from her home in the Lake District.

26 Mrs Beeton, *The Book of Household Management* (London, 1859), p. 695.

27 Carlo Consiglio's argument in *Diane and Minerva* (Rome, 1990).

28 Margaret Magat, 'Fertilised duck eggs and their role in Filipino culture', *Western Folklore* (Spring 2002).

29 'Jin-Ling Black-beaked duck', www.monopause.net/jinlingducksite/ jinlingduck.html (accessed May 2008).

30 Paul Johnsgard, *Ducks, Geese and Swans of the World* (London, 1978), p. 138.

31 *Foie gras entier* is pure liver cooked whole, *pâte de canard* is a mix, *mousceau pâte* is minced, *cou farci* is stuffed neck, *magret farci* is stuffed breast fillet, *magret seche ou fume* is dried or smoked breast fillet, *civet de canard* is jugged duck, *gésiers* are gizzards, *coeurs* are hearts, *rillettes* are potted, *confits* are pickled, *grillons* are grilled and

graisse is duck fat or dripping.

32 *Foie gras* (commonly goose) played a significant role in the culinary
history of Europe's Ashkenazi Jews. Though hard evidence for
Jewish *foie gras* consumption dates back only to the Middle Ages,
the Jews probably assimilated this delicacy during the first century
AD while living under Roman rule, establishing the use of poultry
fat as part of their dietary law. In medieval times children were
given liver before Hanukkah and Passover. When diaspora Jews
began their migration out of Palestine, they carried many of their
food customs with them, including a love for *foie gras* and a
knowledge of how to produce it. Rabbis then and now, writing
about animals raised or slaughtered in an inhumane manner,
suggest it is not possible that *foie gras* could be considered kosher.
Claudia Roden, *The Book of Jewish Food: An Odyssey from Samarkand
to New York* (New York, 1996).

33 Mithridates was king of Pontos (Turkey) about 114–63 BC. H.J.F.
Horstmanshoff, 'Medicament, Magic and Poison in the Roman
Empire', *European Review*, VII/1 (1999), pp. 37–51.

34 'His Majesty the Duck': www.tourdargent.com (accessed 25 July 2007).

35 'The World of Cherry Valley': www.cherryvalley.co.uk (accessed May
2008).

3 THE DUCK'S QUACK

1 Pseudonym of American poet Frederick Petersen, 1859–1938.

2 John Berger, 'Why Look at Animals?', citing Rousseau's *Essay on the
Origin of Languages*, in G. Dyer, ed., *John Berger: Selected Essays*
(London, 2001), p. 261.

3 R. Allen Gardner and B. T. Gardner, 'Teaching Sign Language to a
Chimpanzee', *Science*, 165 (1969), pp. 664–72.

4 Paul Beale, ed., *A Dictionary of Slang and Unconventional English*
(London, 1937), p. 348.

5 George Godfrey, *History of George Godfrey: Written by Himself*
(London, 1828).

6 G. A. Wilkes, *A Dictionary of Australian Colloquialisms* (Sydney, 1978).

7 Geoffrey Chaucer, 'The Parliament of Fowles', in Robert Southey, ed., *Select Works of the British Poets* (London, 1831); 'That men should always love, without cause! Who can find reason or wit in that? Does one who is mirthless dance merrily? . . .'

8 Daniel Defoe, *The Fortunes and Misfortunes of the Famous Moll Flanders* (London, 1750), chap. 39.

9 Charles Dickens, *Barnaby Rudge* (New York, 1842), chap. 8.

10 Charles Dickens, *Pickwick Papers* (Boston, MA, 1868), chap. 34.

11 Charles Dickens, *The Old Curiosity Shop* (London, 1847–52), chap. 11.

12 Letter from Henry VIII to Anne Boleyn, *c.* 1528 – www.geocities.com/boleynfamily/transcripts/henry.html (accessed October 2007) – as an example of the word 'ducky' having changed.

13 J. E. Lighter, ed., *Historical Dictionary of American Slang* (New York, 1994), vol. I, pp. 666–8. Also Beale, *A Dictionary of Slang and Unconventional English*, p. 349.

14 It is difficult to trace any possible links from 'duck' to similar-sounding slang words such as 'fuck' or 'dick' since these were taboo words, therefore not necessarily recorded in early dictionaries; 'dick' used in conjunction with other words as an insult (e.g. 'dickhead') can be traced to British Army slang from 1891, a parallel to the prevalence of military duck slang words and phrases.

15 F. G. Cassidy and R. B. Le Page, *Dictionary of Jamaican English* (Cambridge, 2002).

16 W. Crooke, ed., *Hobson-Jobson: A Glossary of Colloquial Anglo-Indian Words and Phrases and of Kindred Terms, Etymological, Historical, Geographical and Discursive* (London, 1886); Purwannah of Tipoo Sultan, in Logan, *Malabar*, vol. III, p. 125.

17 Farrukh Dhondy, *Bombay Duck* (London, 1990), p. 241.

18 From a verse song in *Comus, a Maske by John Milton presented at Ludlow Castle* (London, 1634).

19 William Shakespeare, *Timon of Athens*, Act IV, Scene 3.

20 B. Bagemihl, *Biological Exuberance: Animal Homosexuality and Natural Diversity* (New York, 1999).

21 Gibson cited in John C. Phillips, *A Natural History of the Ducks*,

4 vols (Boston, MA, 1922–6), vol. I, pp. 128–39.

22 Hall cited in ibid.

23 Millais (1913), cited in Phillips, vol. II, p. 207.

24 Originally 'Old MacDougal had a Farm in O-hi-o-i-o' with associated farm animal noises is described as an army song collected by John Goss for the *Community Song Book* (London, 1927), p. 55. The earliest printing of the song has been traced to October 1917, in *Tommy's Tunes* (London, 1917), a collection of soldiers' songs, marching melodies, rude rhymes and popular parodies. The song shifted to 'Old McDonald's' farm in the 1920s.

25 Virginia Woolf to Margaret Llewelyn Davies, 28 April 1935, cited in the introduction to Leonard Woolf, *Quack, Quack!* (London, 1935).

26 Muriel Spark, *The Ballad of Peckham Rye* [1960] (London, 1963), chap. 5, pp. 65–6, and chap. 9, p. 136.

27 Mozart's K220 Mass has a violin chirping like a bird, hence its nickname *Spatzen Mass* (*Sparrow Mass*). Stravinsky takes on depiction of bird sounds – with tremolos, gruppetti, pizzicato glissandi, string and harp harmonics, and trills – in his *Rite of Spring*, and Satie's work features piano patterns with loons. For Messiaen, see Paul Griffiths, *Olivier Messiaen and the Music of Time* (London, 1985).

28 Such as the 'audio collages' of Peter Pannke's *Opera of Birds* and Walter Tilgner's *Winter at Lake Constance*, making use of digital sound recordings of thousands of diving ducks, pochards, etc., over the last twenty years.

29 John Levack Drever, Notes for *The Quack Project*, CDRom, 2001.

30 Given Stockhausen's work with reverberation, the urban legend that a 'duck's quack has no echo' is interesting. This was finally disproved in 2003. Tested in an anechoic chamber at the University of Salford, Manchester, a duck called Daisy demonstrated her quack – though quiet – had a distinct echo.

31 Karlheinz Stockhausen, *Stockhausen Talks: Hymnen, 1966–67*, sinologic.com/newmusic/sub/hymen.html (accessed November 2001) and www.stockhausen.org. *Hymnen (Anthems) Electronic and Concrete Music with Soloists.*

1 Gaby Wood, *Living Dolls: A Magical History of the Quest for Mechanical Life* (London, 2002), p. 34.

2 After Julien Offrey de la Mettrie published a mechanistic treatise, *The Natural History of the Soul*, in 1747, he lost his job, and all copies of the book were burnt. He is quoted in Wood's *Living Dolls*, pp. 12–13.

3 Ibid., pp. 24–5.

4 Thomas Pynchon, *Mason and Dixon* (London, 1998), and p. 448.

5 Ibid., extracts from pp. 372–83.

6 Steven Watts, *The Magic Kingdom: Walt Disney and the American Way of Life* (Boston, MA, 1997), p. 73.

7 Ibid., p. 181. As mischievous and gregarious as male ducks embarked on sexual antics, the Disney crew – 'Fat Boy' Roy Williams and 'Banana Nose' Jack Kinney were the instigators here. They adored practical jokes, constantly misbehaved at the studio, and threw famously wild parties.

8 Ibid., p. 183.

9 Quoted in Esther Leslie's *Hollywood Flatlands: Animation, Theory and the Avant-Garde* (London, 2002), p. 161.

10 Ariel Dorfman and Armand Mattelart, *How to Read Donald Duck: Imperialist Ideology in the Disney Comic* (New York, 1971), p. 91 and closing lines.

11 Ibid.

12 Robert Pincus-Witten, *Roy Lichtenstein, A Drawing Retrospective*, exh. cat., James Goodman Gallery (New York, 1984), n.p.

13 George Orwell, *Nineteen Eighty-Four* (London, 2003), chap .5.

14 Gottfried Helnwein, 'Memories of Duckburg', in *Donald Duck 70 jaar jong!* (*D. D. 70 Years Young!*), exh. cat. (Amstelveen, Netherlands), pp. 22, 31.

15 This is a homage to (or pastiche of) Magritte's 1930s *This is Not a Pipe* series, which involved a painted pipe with the title words beneath, but in series explored the idea of a thing represented clearly not being the actual thing, including a painting on an easel in front of a window scene which is also a painting, in recursive

infinity. A similarly existential question is asked in Peter Weir's film *The Truman Show* (1998), in which the hero discovers his life is not real but Reality TV and, on trying to escape, reaches the edge of the cardboard set.

5 PLAYING DUCK

1 Konrad Lorenz's assumption that duck displays were instinctive or innate 'fixed action patterns' in his monograph on duck behaviour of 1941, comparing twenty species, was challenged by Lehrman in 1953, who argued that clarifying behaviours is counter-productive since it does not explore how behaviour actually develops and may distract us from finding out. Lehrman's hostile attack had enormous impact. The instinctive versus learned debate continues, expressed now as 'constitutional' versus 'experiential'.

2 Information about NOAA's interest in the bath toys is online at www.afsc.noaa/gov./.

3 Geoff Dyer, ed., *John Berger: Selected Essays* (London, 2001), p. 266.

6 QUACKERY UNMASK'D

1 For example, *The So Much Famed Tablets: A Description of a Quack Medicine* (London, 1680); J. Wiggins, *A Catalogue of Cures: A Collection of 185 advertisements, chiefly relating to quack medicines. The greater part English, the rest French, German and Italian, 1660–1716. An Explanation of the Vices of the Age Shewing The Knavery of Landords, The Imposition of Quack Doctors, The Roguery of Petty-Lawyers, The Cheats of Bum-Bailiffs and the Intrigues of Lewd Women*, Printed and Sold at no. 4, Long Lane, Smithfield, London, dated 1880?; *De Franse Quackslaver of de Boere Klap Beurs* [The French Quack from Clap District] (Groningen, 1689).

2 John Spike, *Quackery Unmasked: A Treatise on Venereal Disease* (London, 1711), n. p.

3 Eric Jameson, *The Natural History of Quackery* (London, 1961), pp. 118–19.

4 Lewis Carroll, *Collected Verse* (London, 1929).

5 Elisabeth Rosenthal, 'Bird Flu Virus May be Spread by Smuggling', *New York Times* (15 June 2006).

6 Janet Kear, *Man and Wildfowl* (London, 1990), p. 218.

7 Organophosphate insecticides inhibit an enzyme (acetylcholinesterase) essential for proper functioning of the nervous system. Because we all have similar mechanisms of nerve transmission, this mode of action is similar in target insects, birds and mammals. Many organophosphates are acutely toxic to birds at very low doses. A recent compilation of acute lethal doses (LD50s) for the mallard duck showed that sixteen to twenty organophosphates were acutely toxic at doses less than 20 mg per kg of body weight and the most toxic had an LD50 over twenty times smaller. Pesticides also cause eggshell thinning. J. K. Bennett, S. E. Dominguez and W. L. Griffis, 'Effects of Dicofol on Mallard Eggshell Quality', *Archives of Environmental Contamination and Toxicology*, XIX/6 (1990), pp. 907–12.

8 Marc Von Roomen and Jesper Madsen, eds, *Waterfowl and Agriculture: Review and Future Perspective of the Crop Damage Conflict in Europe* (Lelystad, Netherlands, 1992), p. 56.

9 Violeta Fuentes Munoz-Pomer, 'Population Genetics and Hybridisation of the White-Headed Duck, *Oxyura leucocephala*, and the Ruddy Duck, *Oxyura jamaicensis*', doctoral thesis, University of Seville, 2005.

10 Animal Aid Director Andrew Tyler's address to a RSPCA seminar examining the fate of the ruddy duck as part of an ongoing campaign against the cull, February 2004.

11 Hans Christian Andersen, 'The Ugly Duckling', in *The Complete Stories* (London, 2005), pp. 201–4.

12 Zdravko Radman, *Metaphors: Figures of the Mind* (London, 1997), p. 151.

13 Born in Gloucestershire, England, F. W. (Will) Harvey was an officer in the First World War. Famously courageous at the front, he did forays alone first to see if it was safe enough to take his men. During one of these, he was caught and made a prisoner of war. On one

occasion, after long solitary confinement, he returned to his bed to find a fellow prisoner had drawn a picture of ducks for him, which inspired the poem 'Ducks'. Decorated for his bravery, Harvey wrote poetry all through the war and after.

14 Monologue on the death of his wife, in William Shakespeare's *Macbeth*, Act v, v.16.

15 Edmund Spenser, 'The Shepherd's Calendar', in *The Shepherd's Calendar and Other Poems* (London, 1978).

16 Jacques Derrida, 'L'Animal que donc je suis (a suivre)', trans. David Wills as 'The Animal That Therefore I Am (More to Follow)', *Critical Inquiry*, 28 (Winter 2002), pp. 369–418.

17 Elias Canetti, *On Crowds and Power* (London, 2000).

18 Discussion between author and child: Author: 'Where do imaginary friends go when we grow up?' Child: 'They turn into ducks and things.'

19 Wallace Stevens, *Opus Posthumous* (New York, 1957).

20 John Berger, 'Why Look at Animals?', in Geoff Dyer, ed., *John Berger: Selected Essays* (London, 2001), p. 266.

21 Gilles Deleuze's and Felix Guattari's three categories: individuated animals or pets, animals with characteristics or attributes, and more demonic animals, from 'A Thousand Plateaus', in *Capitalism and Schizophrenia*, trans. B. Massumi (London, 1988), pp. 239–41.

22 The Tsimshians are First Nation peoples living by the Skeena River, off the north coast of British Columbia and Alaska.

23 Traditional American song for outdoor camps and scouting-type events, sung to the tune of 'Stars and Stripes Forever', covered by Mitch Miller in the 1960s; also on Disney's *The Best of Silly Songs*.

24 Attributed to Sam Goldwyn (1882–1974), speaking in admiration of Shakespeare, in John Gross, *After Shakespeare* (Oxford, 1995).

Bibliography

Andersen, Hans Christian, 'The Ugly Duckling', in *The Complete Stories*, trans. Jean Hersholt (London, 2005)

Bagemihl, Bruce, *Biological Exuberance: Animal Homosexuality and Natural Diversity* (New York, 1999)

Bedard, Michael, *Sitting Ducks* (London, 2001)

Bokonyi, S., 'Definitions of Animal Domestication', in J. Clutton-Brook, ed., *The Walking Larder: Patterns of Domestication, Pastoralism and Predation* (London, 1989)

Colegate, Isobel, *The Shooting Party* (Harmondsworth, 1980)

Dahl, Roald, *The Magic Finger* (London, 1966)

Delacour, Jean, *The Living Air: Memoirs of an Ornithologist* (London, 1966)

Derrida, Jacques, 'The Animal That Therefore I Am (More to Follow)', trans. David Wills, *Critical Inquiry*, 28 (Winter 2002)

Dhondy, Farukh, *Bombay Duck* (London, 1990)

Dorfman, A., and A. Mattelart, *How to Read Donald Duck: Imperialist Ideology in the Disney Comic* (New York, 1971)

Duret, *Histoire admirable des herbes emerveillables* (1605).

Emerson, Ralph Waldo, *Nature: Addresses and Lectures* [1849] (New York, 2004)

Enkell, Pierre, and Pierre Rézeau, *Dictionnaire des onomatopées* (Paris, 2003)

Gerald of Wales, *The History and Topography of Ireland*, trans. John O'Meara (Harmondsworth, 1951)

Goldwasser, Orly, *From Icon to Metaphor* (London, 1995)

Grant, Michael, *Erotic Art in Pompeii: The Secret Collection of the National Museum of Naples* (London, 1975)

Halliwell, J. O., *Dictionary of Archaic and Provincial Words* (London, 1889)

Jameson, Eric, *The Natural History of Quackery* (London, 1961)

Johnsgard, Paul A., *Ducks, Geese and Swans of the World* (London, 1978)

Kear, Janet, *Man and Wildfowl* (London, 1990)

Kroeber, A. L., and R. H. Lowie, *American Archeology and Ethnography*, vol. xxv (1929)

Leslie, Esther, *Hollywood Flatlands: Animation, Critical Theory and the Avant-garde* (London, 2002)

Lévi-Strauss, Claude, *Mythologiques (Introduction to a Science of Mythology): The Raw and the Cooked* (London, 1970)

—, *The Way of Masks* (London, 1982).

Lighter, J. E, ed., *Historical Dictionary of American Slang*, vol. 1 (New York, 1994)

Mackenty, John G., *Duck Hunting* (London, 1964)

Magat, Margaret, 'Balut: Fertilized Duck Eggs and their Role in Filipino Culture', *Western Folklore* (Spring 2002)

Mitchell, W. T., *Picture Theory* (Chicago, 1994)

Phillips, John C., *A Natural History of the Ducks*, 4 vols (Boston, MA, 1922–6)

Potter, Beatrix, *Jemima Puddleduck* [1908] (London, 2002)

Pynchon, Thomas, *Mason and Dixon* (London, 1998)

Prejevalsky, Colonel N., *From Kulja, across the Tian Shan to Lob-Nor*, trans. E. Delmar (London, 1879)

Ransome, Arthur, *Peter Duck* (London, 1932)

Richard, Frances, 'Fifteen Theses on the Cute', *Cabinet Magazine*, no. 4, *Immaterial Incorporated* (Summer 2001)

Salisbury, Joyce E., *The Beast Within* (London, 1994)

Scieska, Jon, and Lane Smith, *The Stinky Cheeseman and Other Fairly Stupid Tales* (London, 1993)

Scollins, R., and J. Titford, *Ey Up Mi Duck: An Affectionate Look at the Speech, History and Folklore of Ilkeston and the Erewash Valley* (Ilkston, 1976)

Spark, Muriel, *The Ballad of Peckham Rye* (London, 1960)
Todd, Frank S., *Natural History of the Waterfowl* (San Diego, 1996)
Tomlinson, David, *Ducks* (London, 1996)
Velthuijs, Max, *'Frog in Love' and 'Frog and Duck'* (London, 1999)
Waddell, Martin, and Helen Oxenbury, *Farmer Duck* (London, 1991)
Watts, Steven, *The Magic Kingdom: Walt Disney and the American Way of Life* (Boston, MA, 1997)
Willcock, Colin, *Duck Shooting* (London, 1962)
Wood, Gaby, *Living Dolls: A Magical History of the Quest for Mechanical Life* (London, 2002)
Wright, Bruce S., *Black Duck Spring* (New York, 1966)
Zheleznova, Irina, *The White Duck*: *A Russian Fairy-tale, Retold in English* (Moscow, 1977)

Associations and Websites

BRITISH TRUST FOR ORNITHOLOGY
www.bto.org

BRITISH WATERFOWL ASSOCIATION
www.waterfowl.org.uk

CARTOON ANIMATION ARCHIVES
toolooney.goldenagecartoons.com/daffy.html
Disney.go.com/vault/archives.donald.html

COALITION AGAINST DUCK SHOOTING
www.duck.org.au

CONSERVATION TODAY, WETLANDS FOR TOMORROW
www.ducks.org

DUCK BIOLOGICS RESEARCH LABORATORY AT CORNELL UNIVERSITY,
NEW YORK
www.duckhealth.com/ducklab.html

DUCK BREEDING
www.duckeggs.com

DUCK STAMPS PROGRAMME
www.fws.gov/duckstamps

GLOBAL GLOSSARY OF QUACKS
www.georgetown.edu/eball/animals/duck.html

INDIAN RUNNER DUCK ASSOCIATION
www.runnerduck.net

INTERNATIONAL WILD WATERFOWL ASSOCIATION (IWWA)
www.greatnorthern.net/~dye/iwwa.html

LE SITE OFFICIEL DES PROFESSIONNELS DU FOIE GRAS
www.lefoiegras.fr

PACIFIC FLYWAY DECOY ASSOCIATION
www.pacificflyway.org

RUBBER DUCK COLLECTIONS AND COMMUNITY FORUM
www.duckplanet.com

SEA DUCK JOINT VENTURE
www.seaduckjv.org

SLIMBRIDGE WETLAND RESERVE
www.wwt.org.uk/visit/slimbridge

TOUR D'ARGENT RESTAURANT
www.tourdargent.com

VAUCANSON RESEARCH
www.swarthmore.edu/Humanities/pschmid1/essays/pynchon
/vaucanson.html

VEGETARIANS INTERNATIONAL VOICE FOR ANIMALS
www.viva.org.uk/campaigns/ducks

WILDFOWLING MAGAZINE
www.wildfowling.co.uk

WWT WILDFOWL AND WETLANDS TRUST
www.wwt.org.uk

ZOOLOGICAL MUSEUM AT TRING
www.nhm.ac.uk/tring/index.html

Acknowledgements

Thanks to the AHRC for gamely awarding me a grant for sabbatical research leave and Richard Andrews for his appreciation and support of the playfully serious.

Special thanks must go to colleagues at Middlesex University and CLE for being such ducks and passing on useful references; the Spitalfields and Isle of Dogs City Farms; Mark Adams, skin specialist in the Bird Group at Tring; Jane Burkinshaw, Curator of Ethnography at the Royal Albert Memorial Museum at Exeter; Mike Lawson-Smith at Hotel Haddock; Hatice Abdullah; Gavin Baldwin; Ron Hammond; Howard Hollands; Blott Krebb; Martin McCabe; Lene Østermark-Johansen; Mark and Rebecca Sinker; David Vigay; Lisa Wigham; Theresa Lane for braving gavage and caring for lame duck Delboy with John Earl and Suzy Humphries; all the de Rijke flock, especially Ralph and Raphaëlla for bringing me a timely duck work ethic and Jean-Luc and Martine for laying duck's table; Elodie Maire for her duck drawings; Heiko Schlombach for the raw and the cooked; and Lord Love a Duck, la Drôme.

Photo Acknowledgements

The author and publishers wish to express their thanks to the below sources of illustrative material and/or permission to reproduce it. (Some sources uncredited in the captions for reasons of brevity are also given below.)

Photos by the author: pp. 14, 86, 98, 113 (top), 147; image courtesy of the author (© Kahve-Society): p. 112; photo Erwin and Peggy Bauer/ US Fish & Wildlife Service: p. 27 (foot); photo Don Becker/US Fish & Wildlife Service: p. 150; Bibliothèque Nationale de France, Paris (Département des Monnaies, Médailles et Antiques): p. 162; photo R. J. Bridges/US Fish & Wildlife Service: p. 67; British Museum, London (photos British Museum Images, © The Trustees of the British Museum): pp. 53, 73, 130 (top), 131 (top); photos Edward S. Curtis/ Library of Congress, Washington, DC (Prints and Photographs Division; Edward S. Curtis Collection): pp. 54, 66; photos Donna Dewhurst/US Fish & Wildlife Service: pp. 26, 47 (top); photo Brent Esmil/US Fish & Wildlife Service: p. 152 (top); photos Milton Friend/US Fish & Wildlife Service: pp. 34, 57; photo George Gentry/US Fish & Wildlife Service: p. 37 (foot); photo courtesy iwasfixin2: p. 37 (top); photo © Marjorie Kibby: p. 14 (foot); photo William Larned/US Fish & Wildlife Service: p. 30; photo courtesy of Kevin McCraken: p. 41; photo Matthew Maran (mattmaran.com): p. 21; photos Dave Menke/US Fish & Wildlife Service: pp. 6, 32, 47 (middle); Musée du Louvre, Paris: pp. 49, 130 (foot); photo National Weather Service (National Oceanic Atmospheric Administration): p. 27 (top); photo courtesy New York Public Library: p. 97; from Ralph Payne-Gallwey, *Book of Duck Decoys* (1894): p. 56;

Index